CRIMINAL MACABRE ™

SPIRIT OF THE DEMON

CRIMINAL MACABRE™

SPIRIT OF THE DEMON

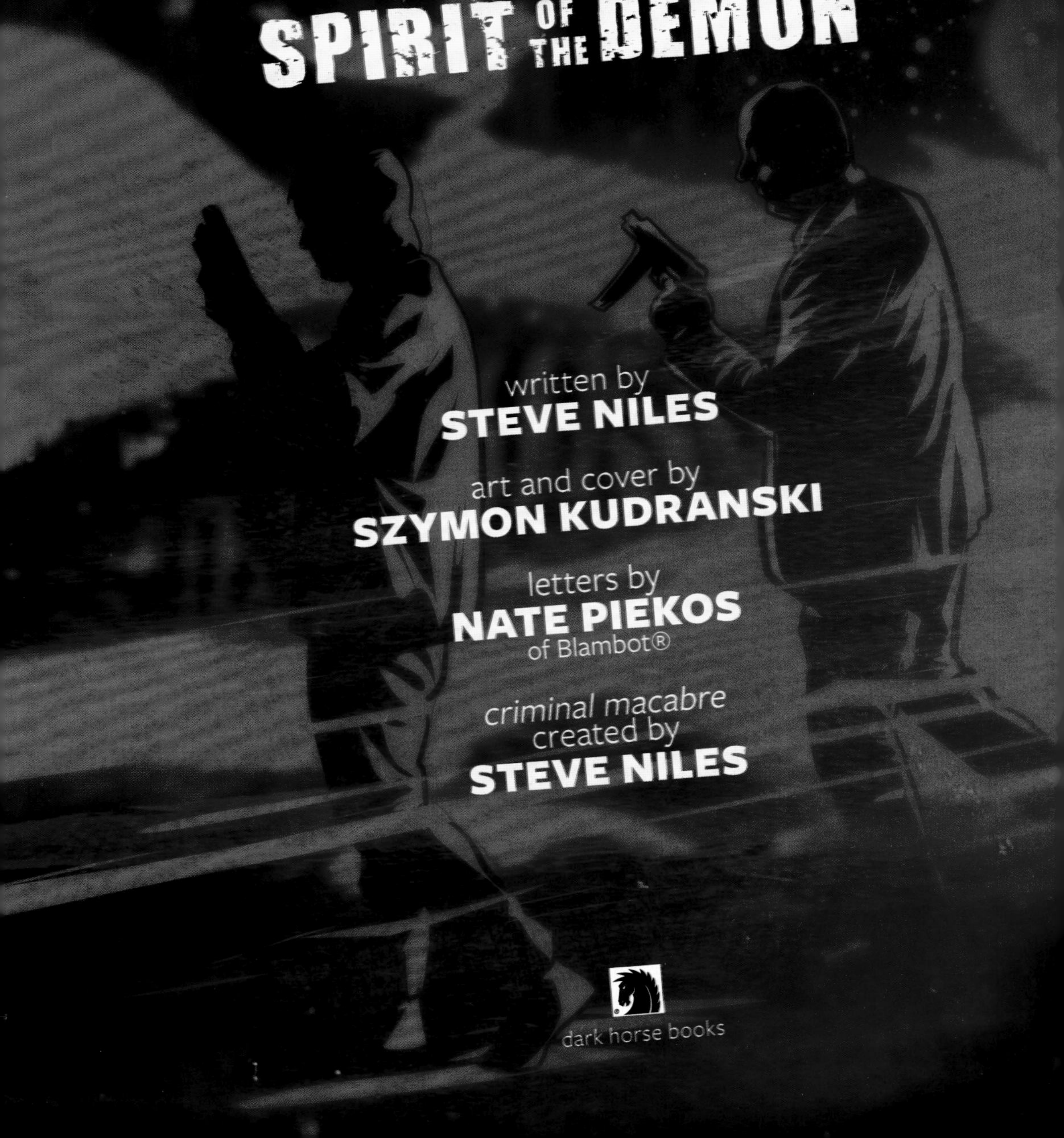

written by
STEVE NILES

art and cover by
SZYMON KUDRANSKI

letters by
NATE PIEKOS
of Blambot®

criminal macabre
created by
STEVE NILES

dark horse books

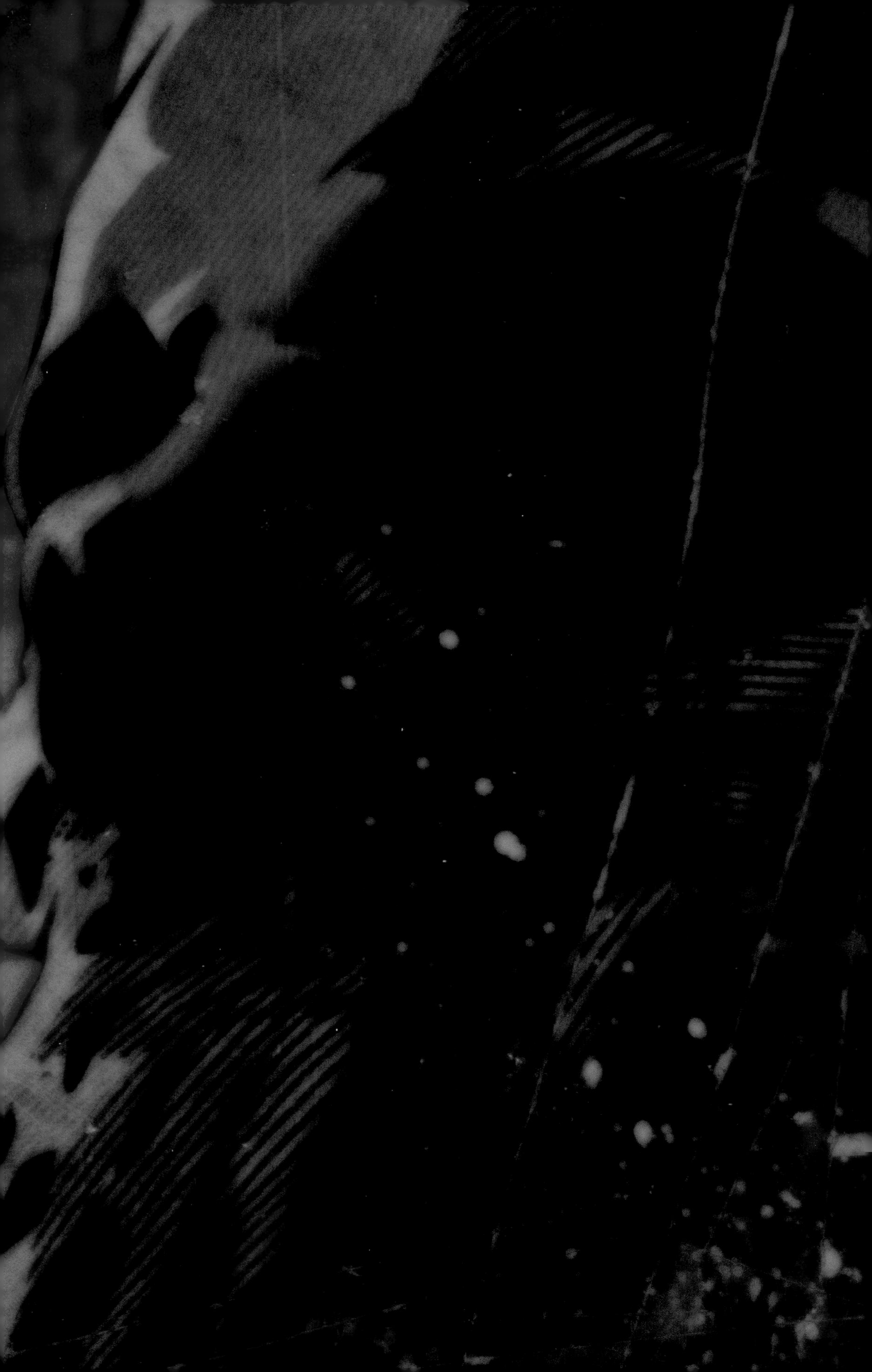

president & publisher
MIKE RICHARDSON

editor
DANIEL CHABON

assistant editors
CHUCK HOWITT and **MISHA GEHR**

designer
PATRICK SATTERFIELD

digital art technician
JOSIE CHRISTENSEN

Published by
DARK HORSE BOOKS
A division of Dark Horse Comics LLC
10956 SE Main Street
Milwaukie, OR 97222

DarkHorse.com

To find a comics shop in your area, visit comicshoplocator.com

FSC MIX Paper from responsible sources FSC® C169962

First edition: July 2022
Ebook ISBN 978-1-50672-988-6
Trade Paperback ISBN 978-1-50672-987-9

10 9 8 7 6 5 4 3 2 1
Printed in China

CRIMINAL MACABRE: SPIRIT OF THE DEMON

Collects the original graphic novel *Criminal Macabre: Spirit of the Demon*

Library of Congress Cataloging-in-Publication Data

Names: Niles, Steve, writer. | Kudranski, Szymon, artist. | Piekos, Nate, letterer.
Title: Criminal macabre : spirit of the demon / written by Steve Niles ; art and cover by Szymon Kudranksi ; letters by Nate Piekos of Blambot.
Description: First edition. | Milwaukie, OR : Dark Horse Books, 2022. | Summary: "Supernatural detective Cal McDonald, is ripped again from his self-imposed retirement to resume his monster-killing career after hunting down a serial-killing priest with a blood-draining knife on a trail leading him directly to the gates of Hell!"-- Provided by publisher.
Identifiers: LCCN 2021059189 (print) | LCCN 2021059190 (ebook) | ISBN 9781506729879 (trade paperback) | ISBN 9781506729886 (ebook)
Subjects: LCGFT: Detective and mystery comics. | Paranormal comics. | Horror comics. | Graphic novels.
Classification: LCC PN6727.N55 C75 2022 (print) | LCC PN6727.N55 (ebook) | DDC 741.5/973--dc23/eng/20220207
LC record available at https://lccn.loc.gov/2021059189
LC ebook record available at https://lccn.loc.gov/2021059190

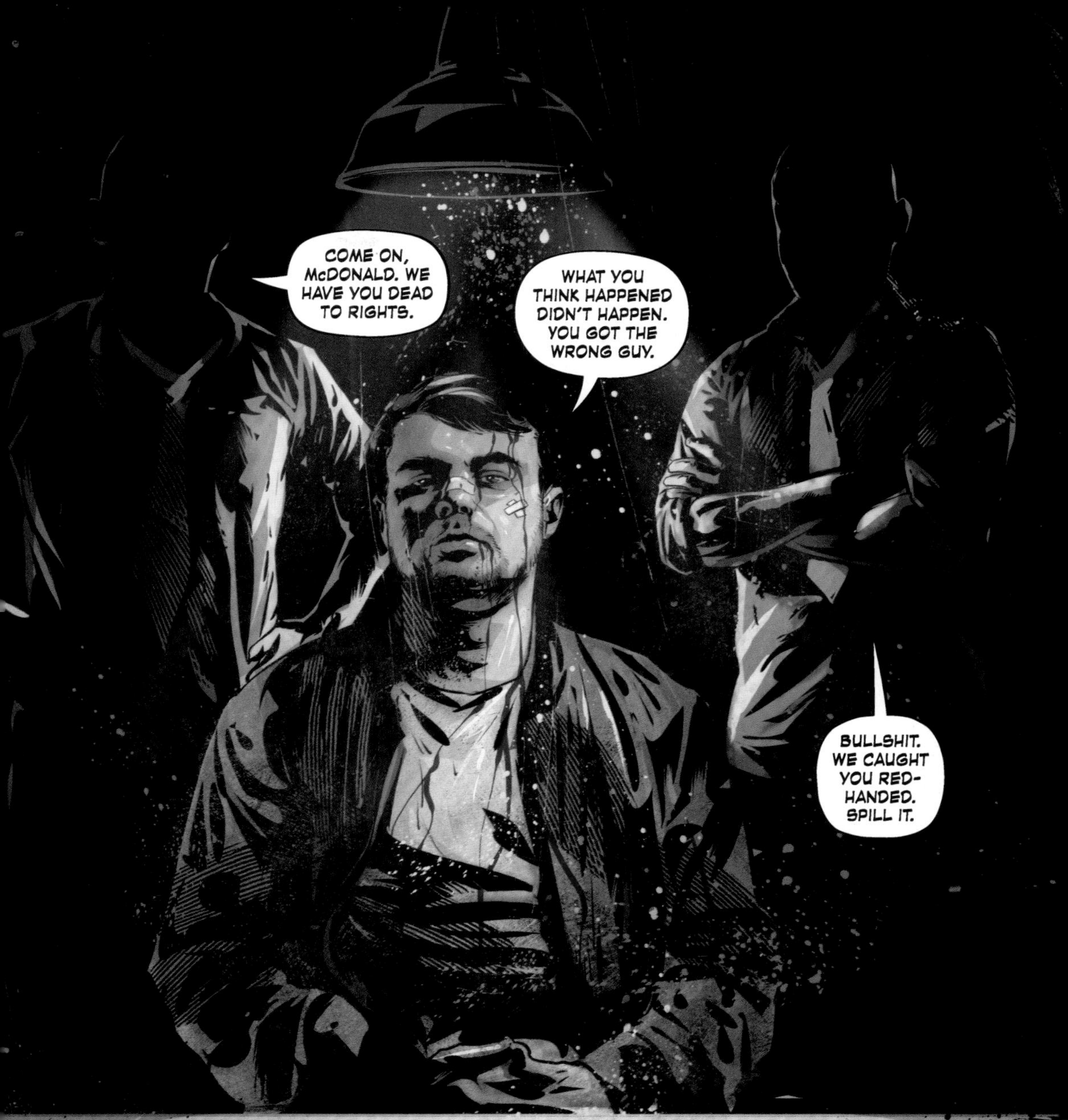
COME ON, McDONALD. WE HAVE YOU DEAD TO RIGHTS.
WHAT YOU THINK HAPPENED DIDN'T HAPPEN. YOU GOT THE WRONG GUY.
BULLSHIT. WE CAUGHT YOU RED-HANDED. SPILL IT.

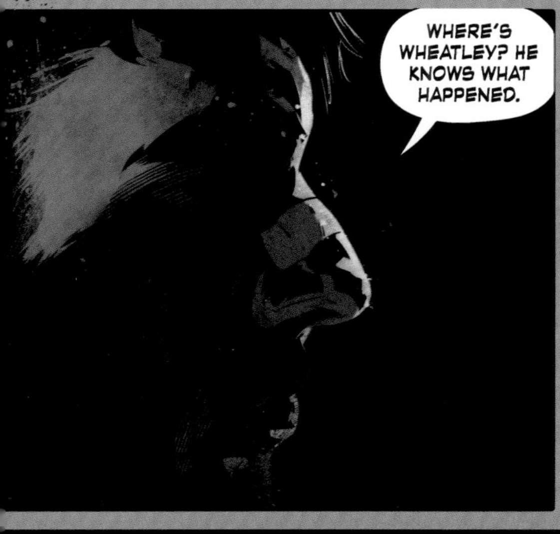
WHERE'S WHEATLEY? HE KNOWS WHAT HAPPENED.

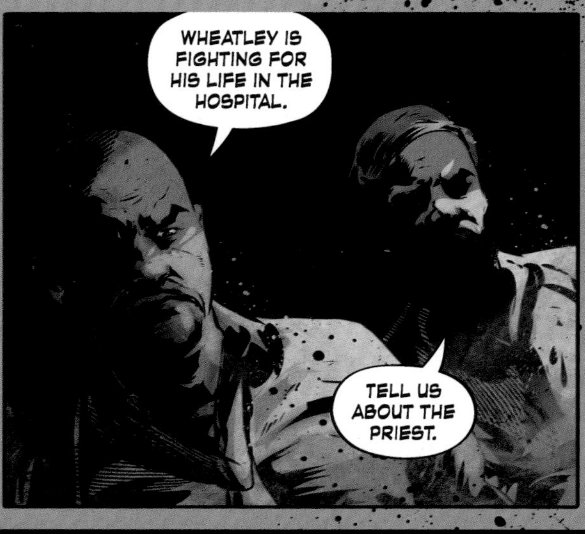
WHEATLEY IS FIGHTING FOR HIS LIFE IN THE HOSPITAL.
TELL US ABOUT THE PRIEST.

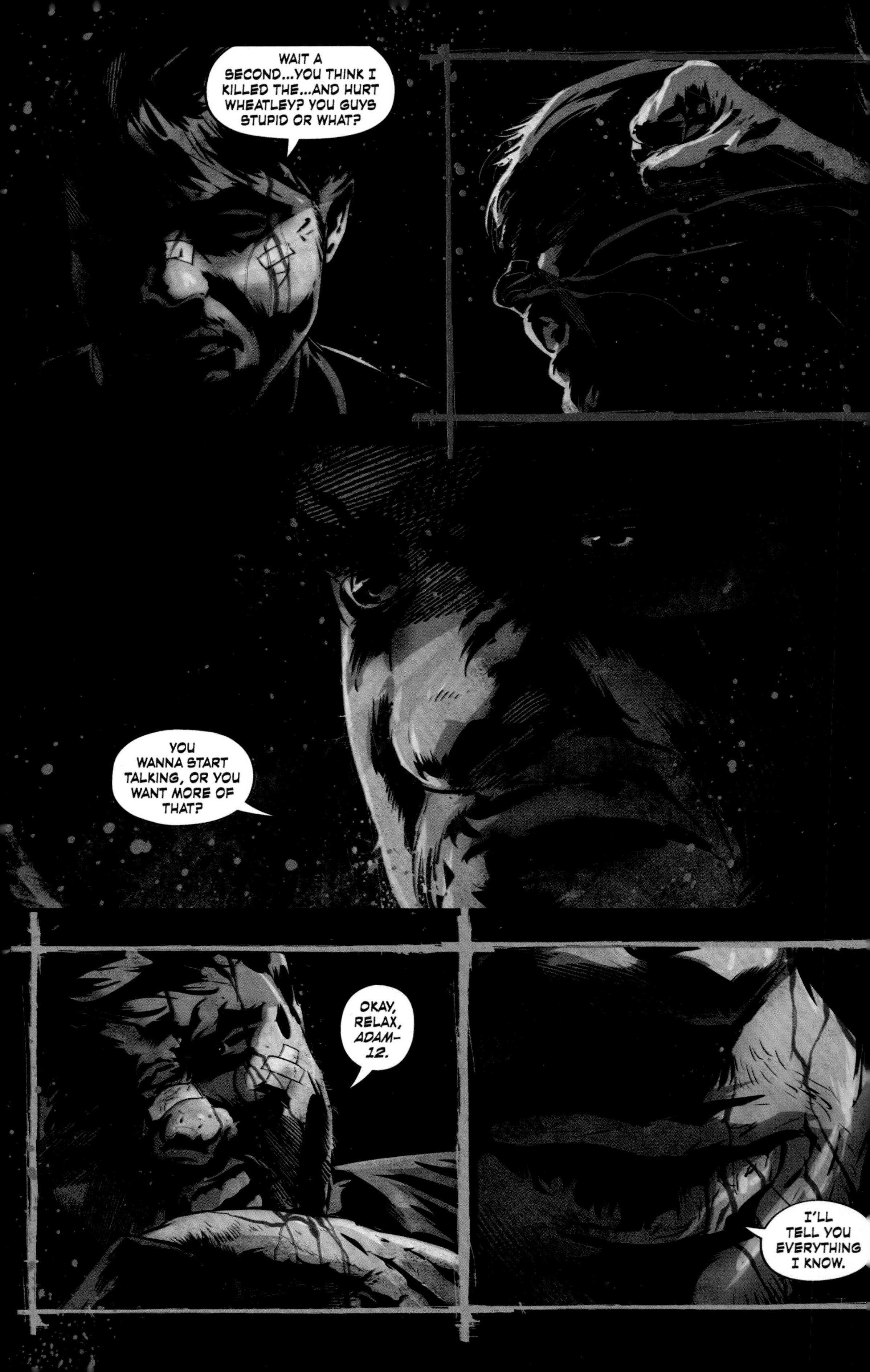
WAIT A SECOND...YOU THINK I KILLED THE...AND HURT WHEATLEY? YOU GUYS STUPID OR WHAT?
YOU WANNA START TALKING, OR YOU WANT MORE OF THAT?
OKAY, RELAX, *ADAM-12.*
I'LL TELL YOU EVERYTHING I KNOW.

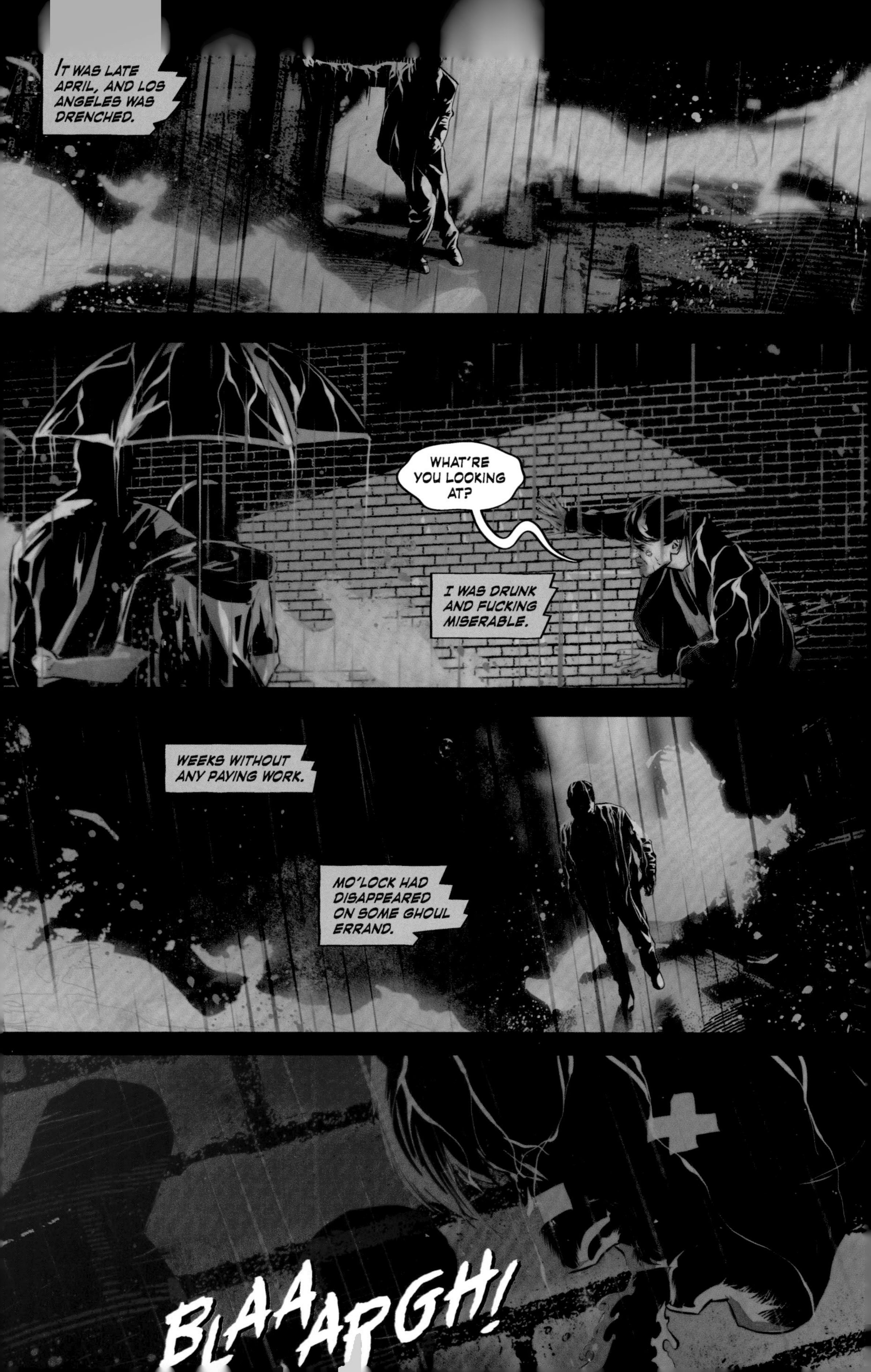
IT WAS LATE APRIL, AND LOS ANGELES WAS DRENCHED.
WHAT'RE YOU LOOKING AT?
I WAS DRUNK AND FUCKING MISERABLE.
WEEKS WITHOUT ANY PAYING WORK.
MO'LOCK HAD DISAPPEARED ON SOME GHOUL ERRAND.
BLAAARGH!

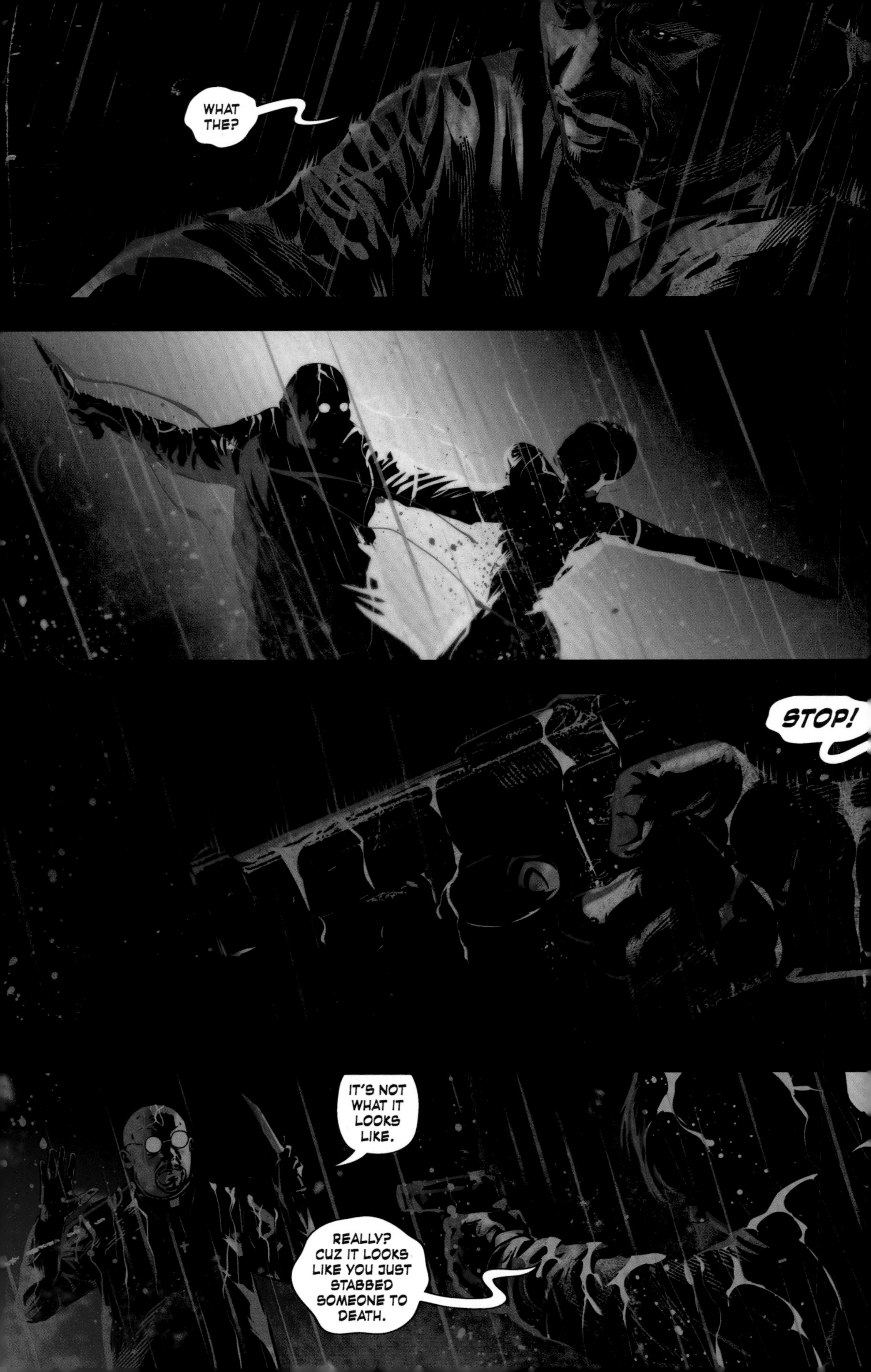
WHAT THE?
STOP!
IT'S NOT WHAT IT LOOKS LIKE.
REALLY? CUZ IT LOOKS LIKE YOU JUST STABBED SOMEONE TO DEATH.

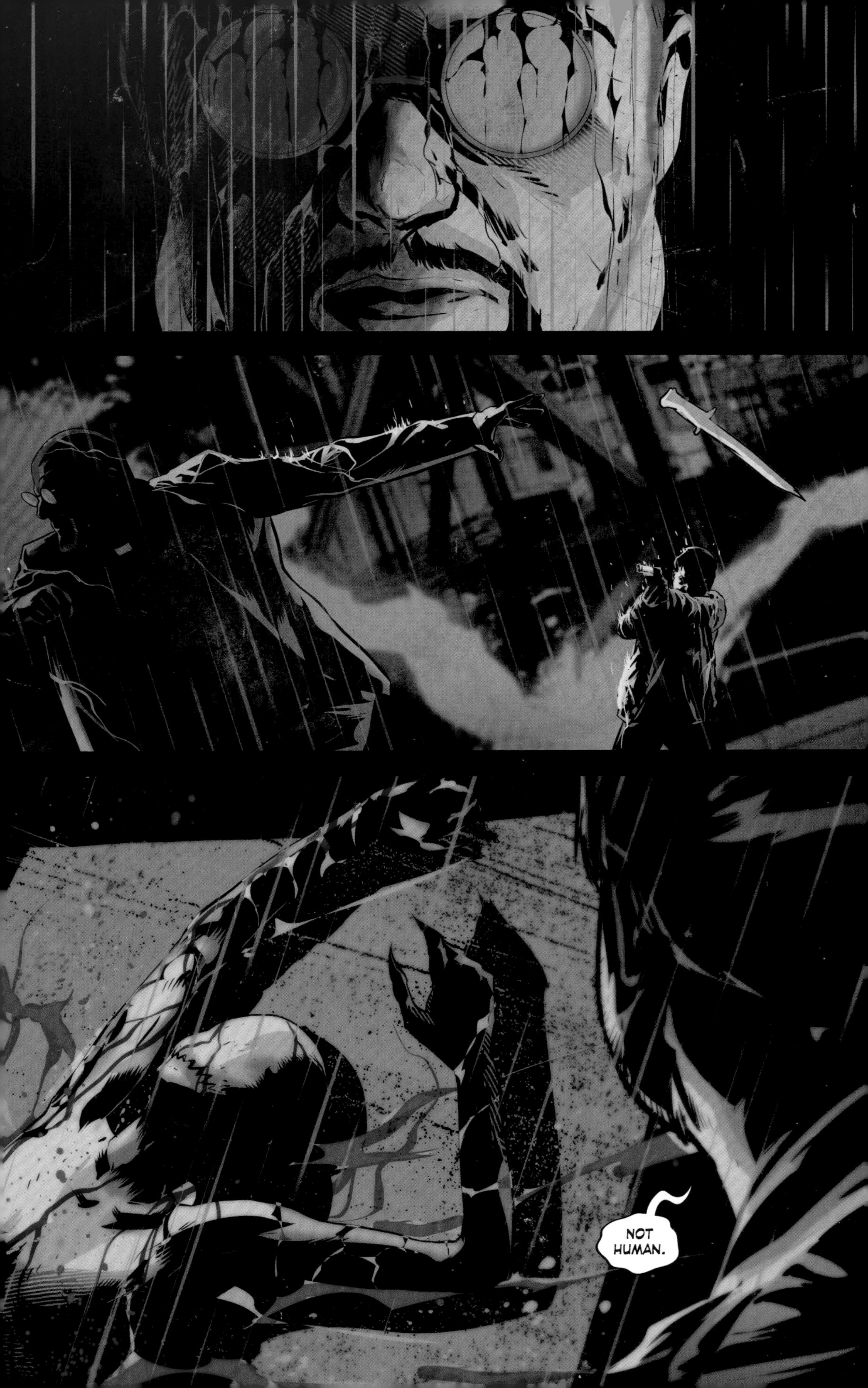
NOT HUMAN.

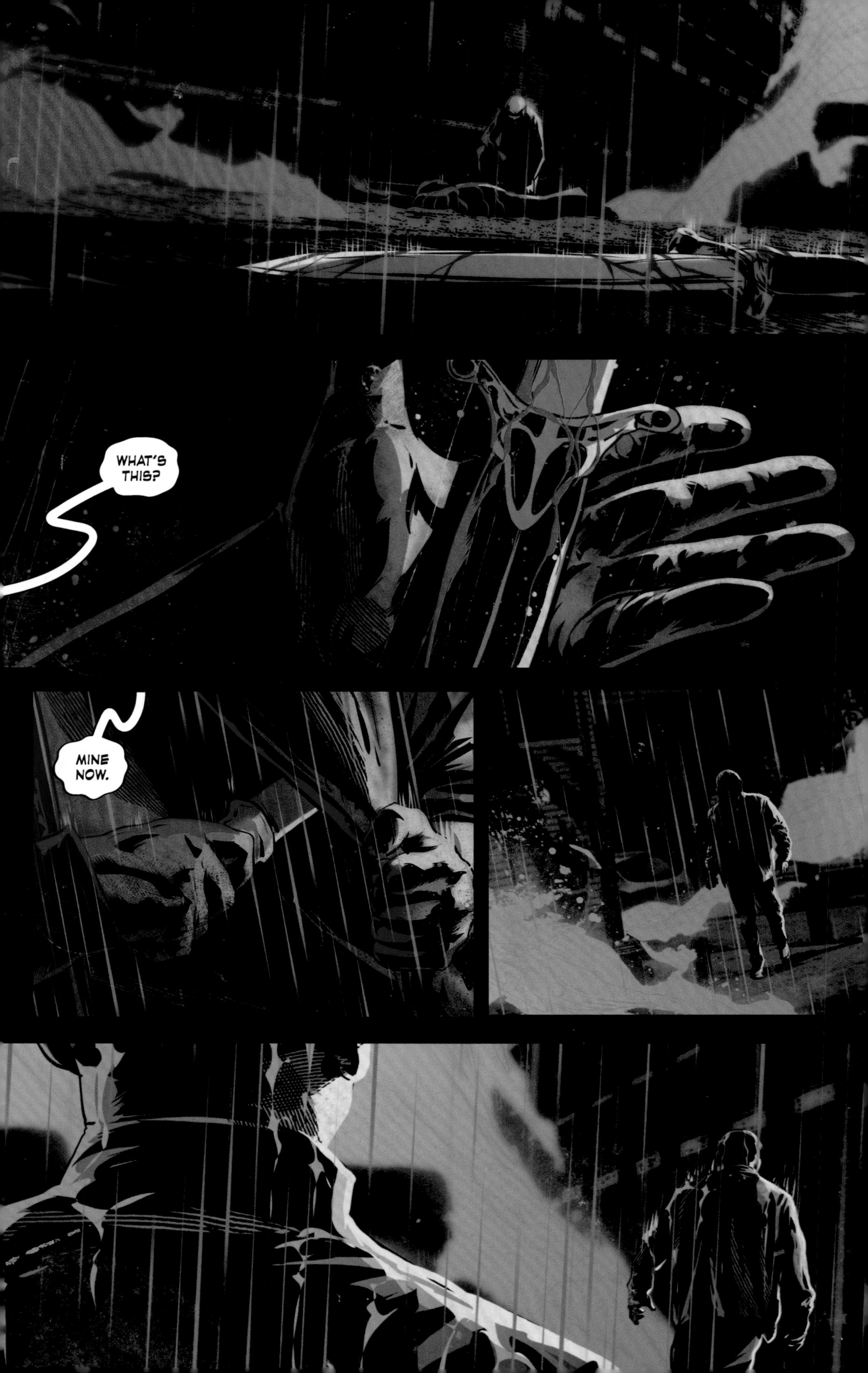
WHAT'S THIS?
MINE NOW.

I HAD TO ADMIT. I WAS PERPLEXED.

PRIEST KILLS MONSTER. PRIEST RUNS AWAY, BUT WHY RUN AWAY?

NOTHING WRONG WITH KILLING MONSTERS, NOT IN MY BOOK AT LEAST.

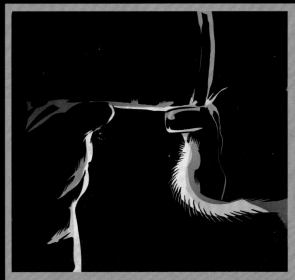

THE KNIFE USED TO KILL THE FREAK WAS OBVIOUSLY ANCIENT AND PROBABLY A SACRIFICIAL WEAPON. LOOKED LIKE A REAL RELIC.

IT HAD A DRAIN FOR BLOOD SO WHEN SOMEONE IS STABBED, THE BLOOD POURS OUT THE END OF THE HANDLE. GRIM SHIT.

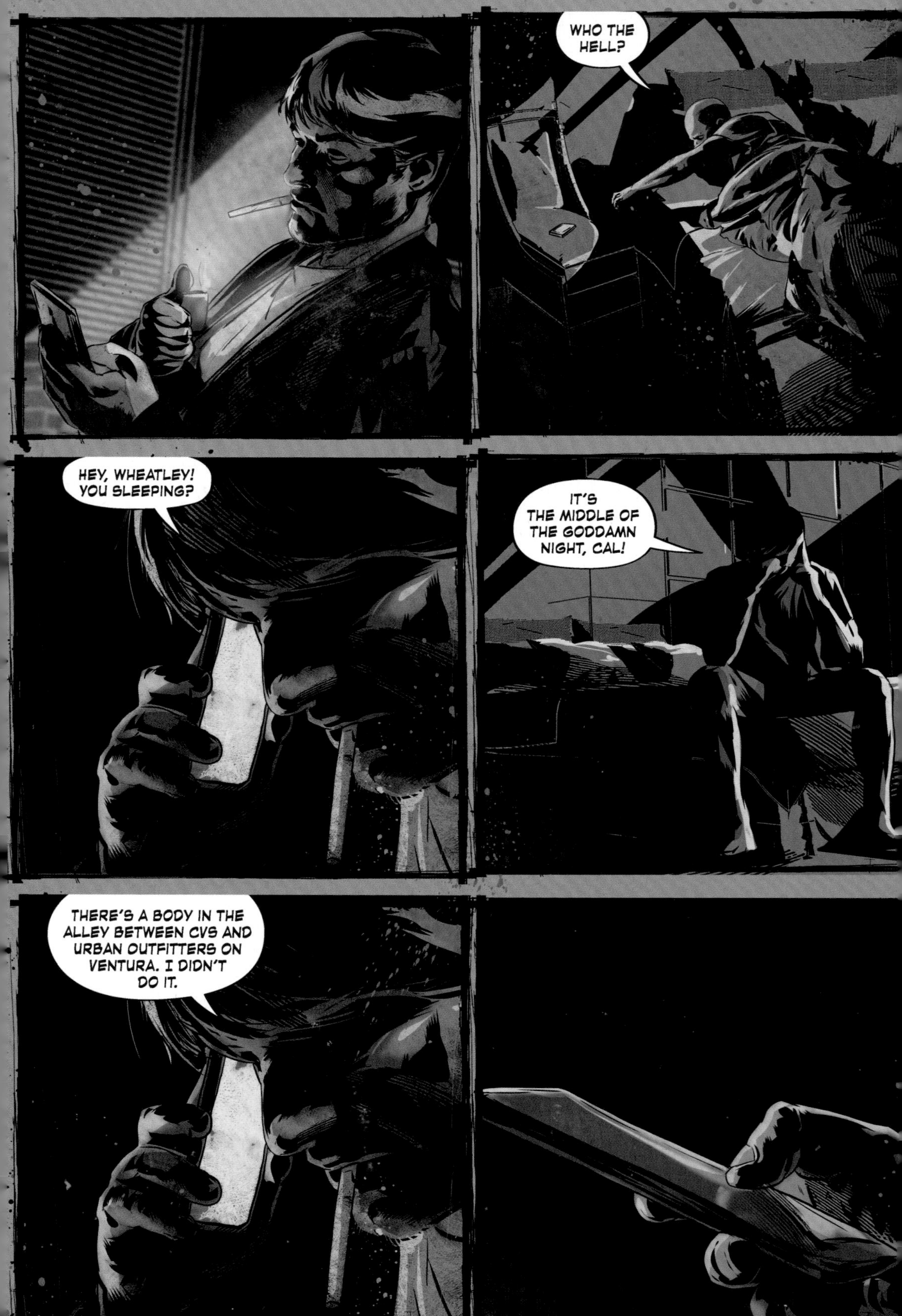
WHO THE HELL?
HEY, WHEATLEY! YOU SLEEPING?
IT'S THE MIDDLE OF THE GODDAMN NIGHT, CAL!
THERE'S A BODY IN THE ALLEY BETWEEN CVS AND URBAN OUTFITTERS ON VENTURA. I DIDN'T DO IT.

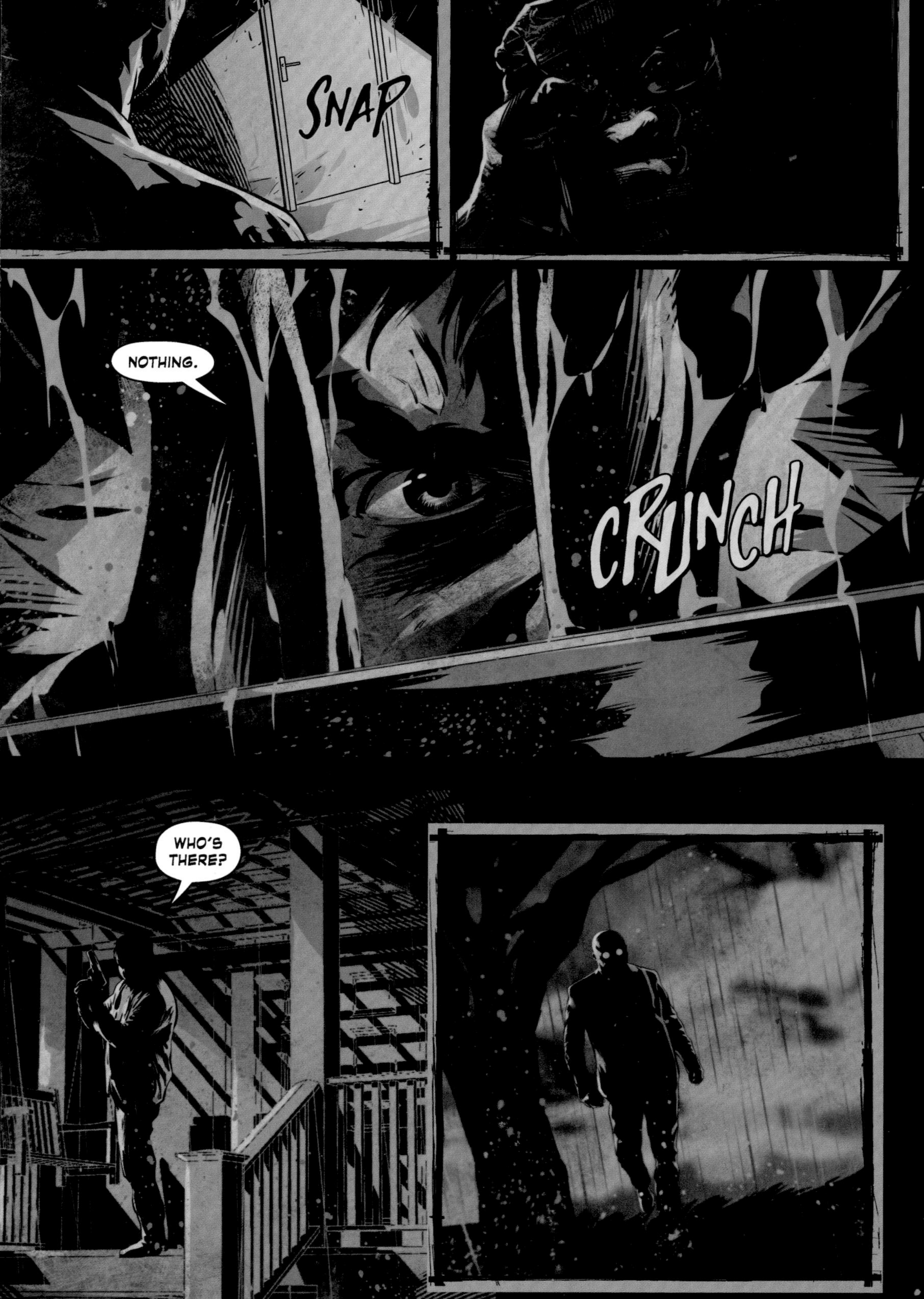
SNAP
NOTHING.
CRUNCH
WHO'S THERE?

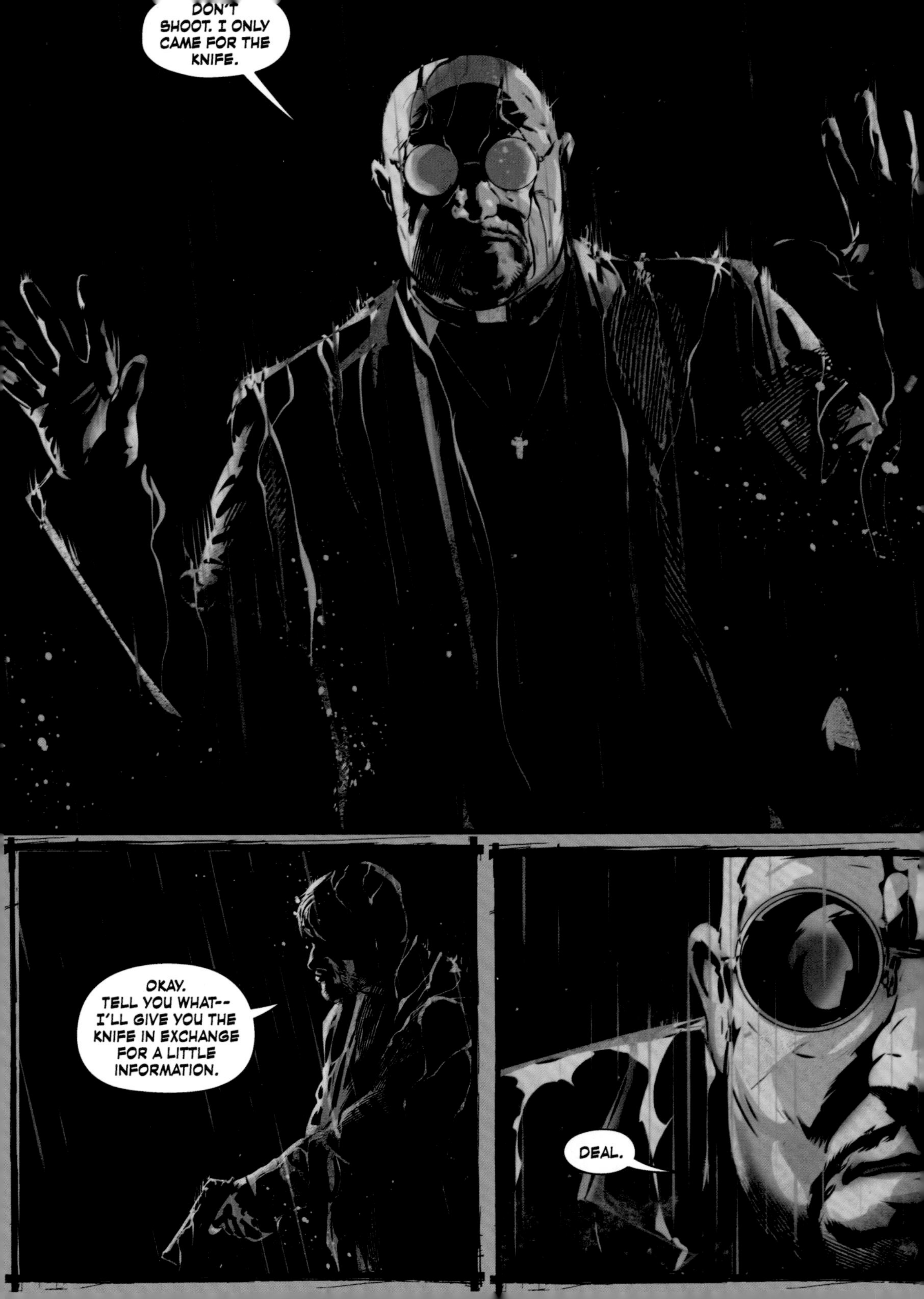
DON'T SHOOT. I ONLY CAME FOR THE KNIFE.
OKAY. TELL YOU WHAT-- I'LL GIVE YOU THE KNIFE IN EXCHANGE FOR A LITTLE INFORMATION.
DEAL.

HAVE A SEAT. CAN I GET YOU A DRINK?

NO THANK YOU. I WON'T BE LONG.

YOU WANT TO TELL ME WHAT HAPPENED IN THE ALLEY?

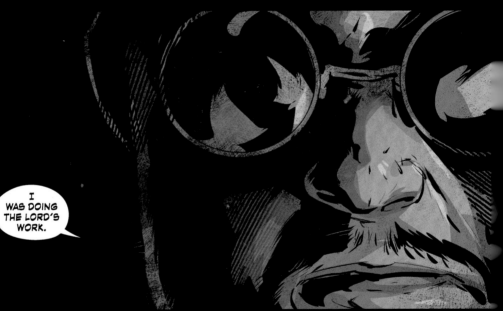

I WAS DOING THE LORD'S WORK.

CAN YOU BE A LITTLE MORE SPECIFIC? I SAW THAT THING YOU KILLED. THAT WAS NOT HUMAN.

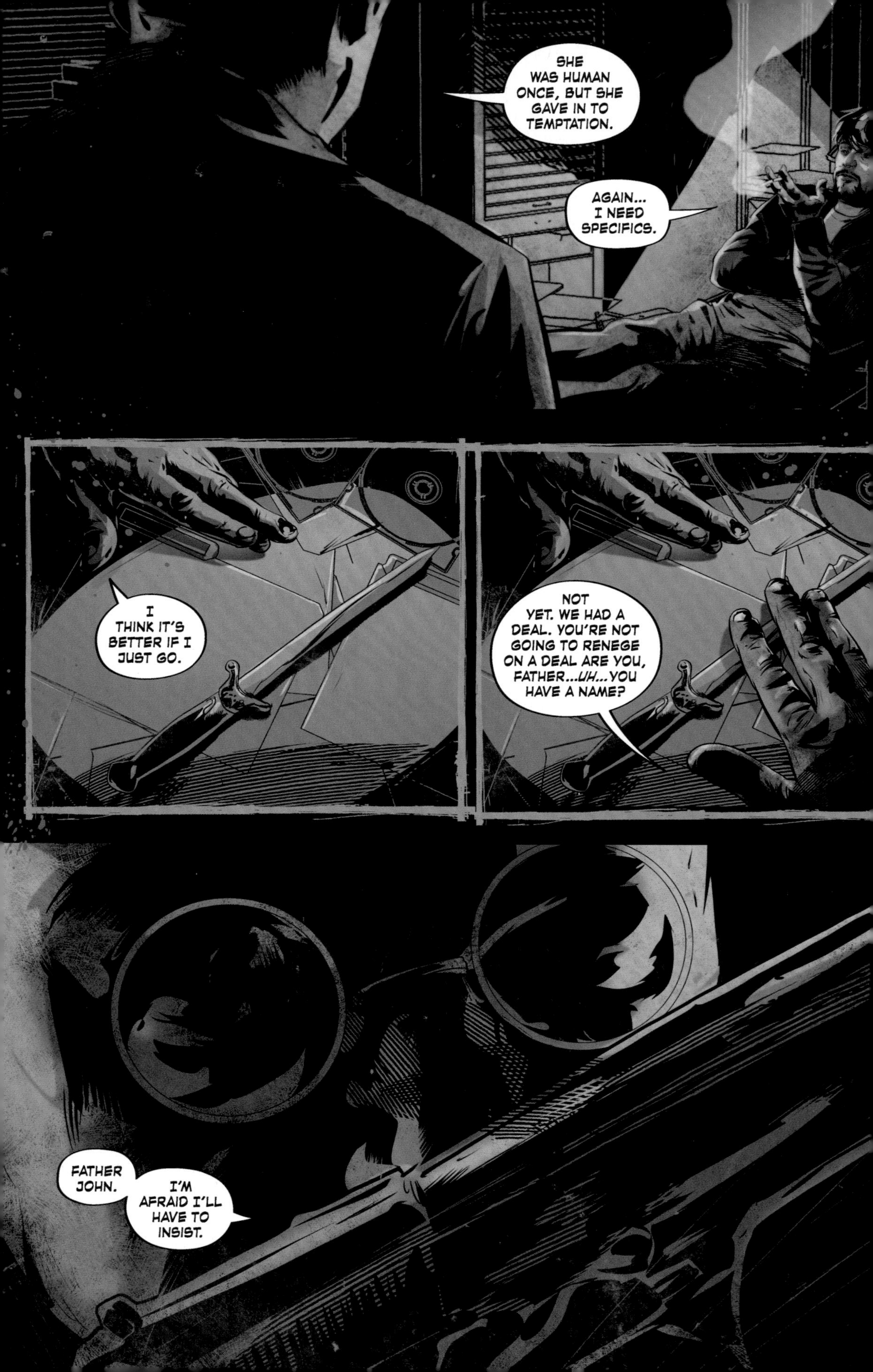
SHE WAS HUMAN ONCE, BUT SHE GAVE IN TO TEMPTATION.
AGAIN... I NEED SPECIFICS.
I THINK IT'S BETTER IF I JUST GO.
NOT YET. WE HAD A DEAL. YOU'RE NOT GOING TO RENEGE ON A DEAL ARE YOU, FATHER...*UH*...YOU HAVE A NAME?
FATHER JOHN.
I'M AFRAID I'LL HAVE TO INSIST.

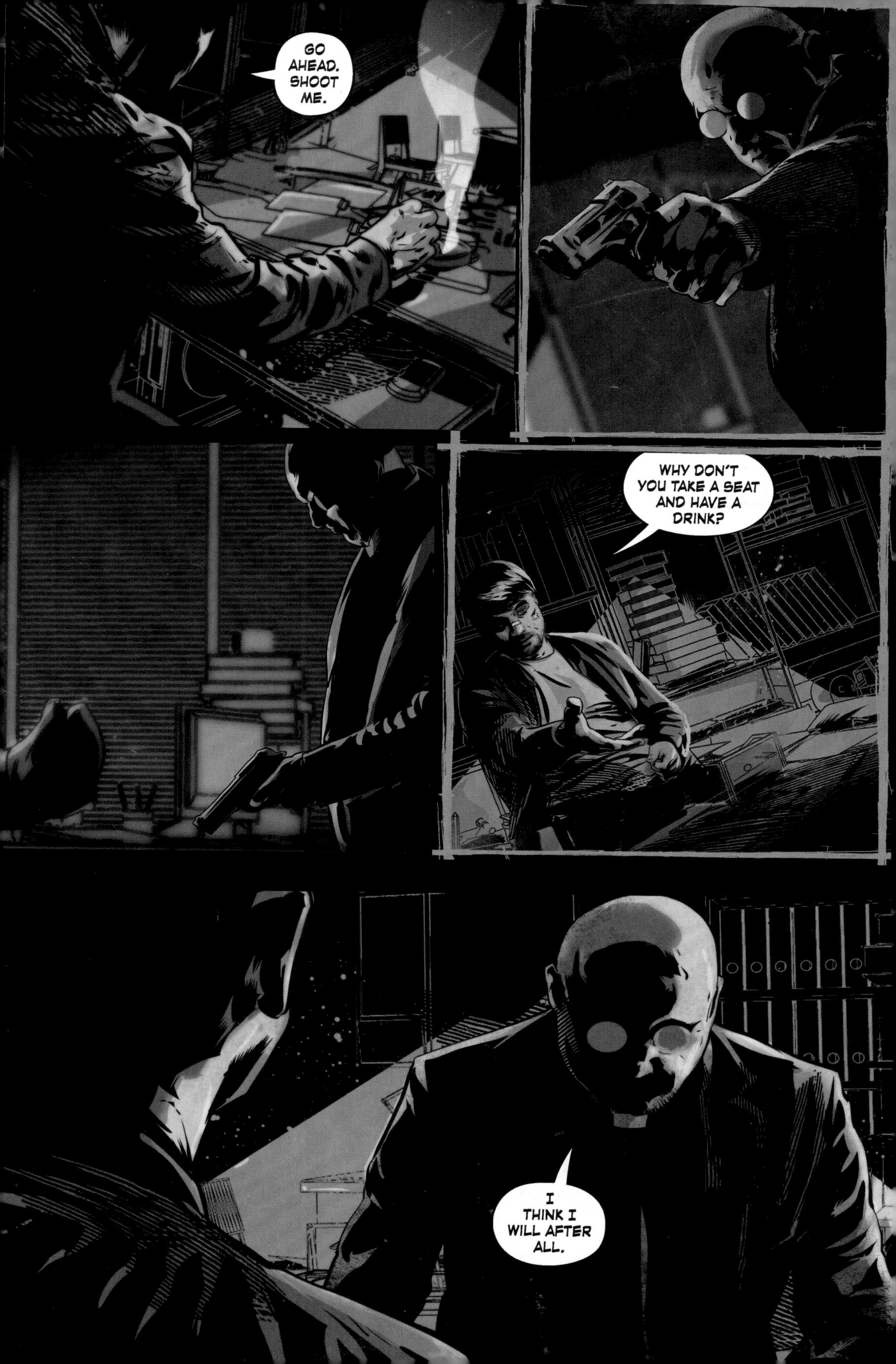
GO AHEAD. SHOOT ME.
WHY DON'T YOU TAKE A SEAT AND HAVE A DRINK?
I THINK I WILL AFTER ALL.

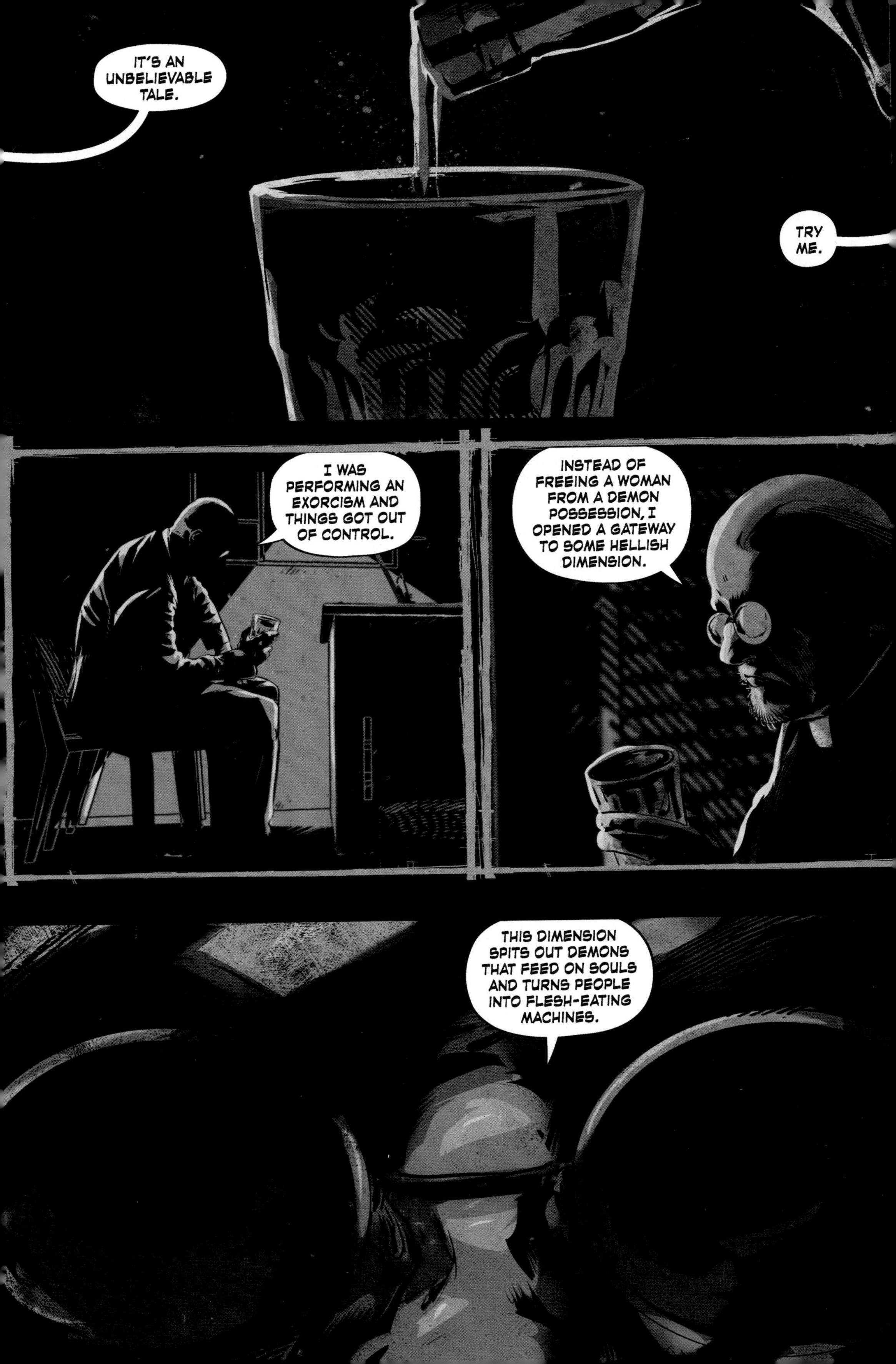
IT'S AN UNBELIEVABLE TALE.
TRY ME.
I WAS PERFORMING AN EXORCISM AND THINGS GOT OUT OF CONTROL.
INSTEAD OF FREEING A WOMAN FROM A DEMON POSSESSION, I OPENED A GATEWAY TO SOME HELLISH DIMENSION.
THIS DIMENSION SPITS OUT DEMONS THAT FEED ON SOULS AND TURNS PEOPLE INTO FLESH-EATING MACHINES.

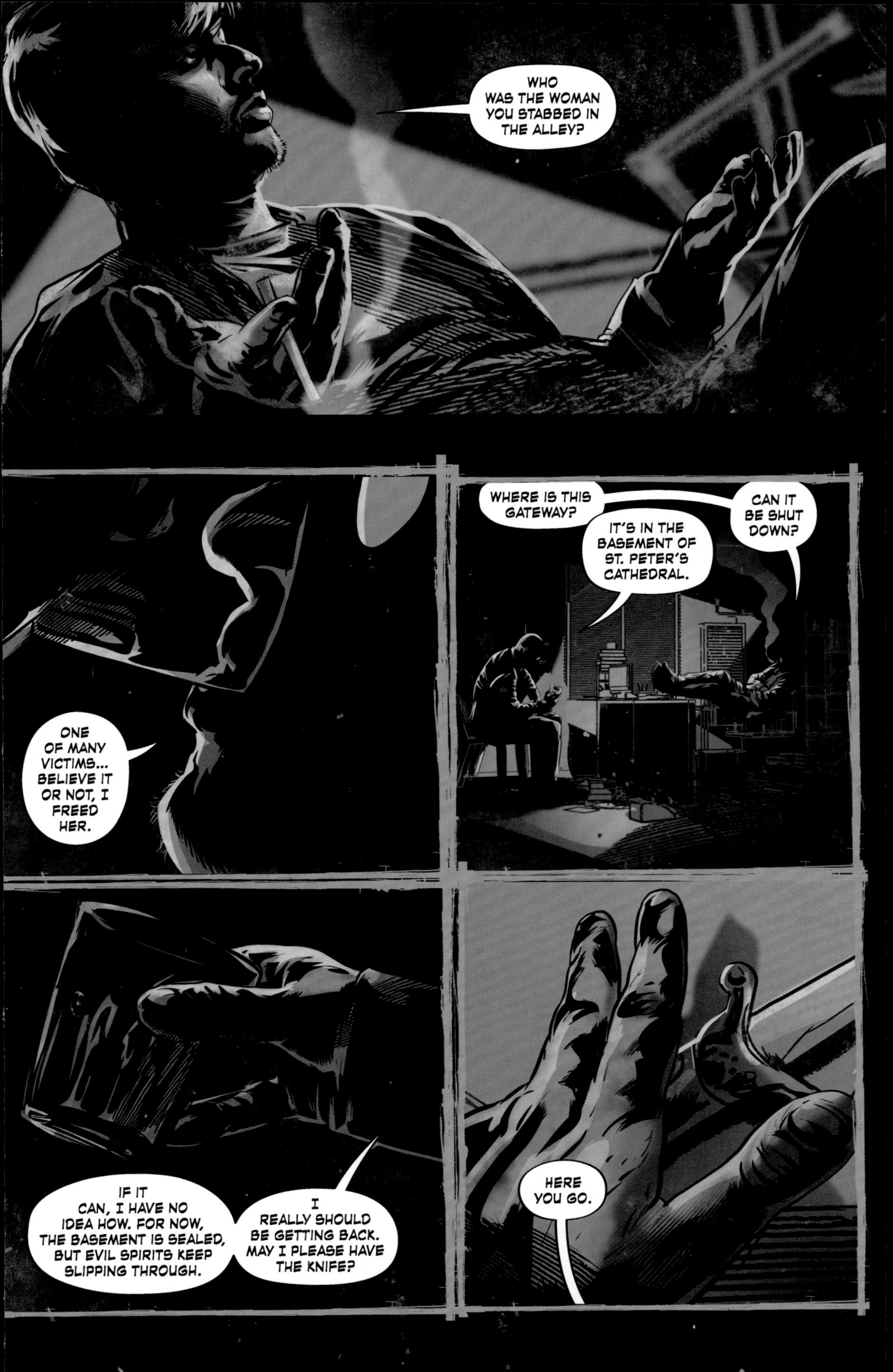
WHO WAS THE WOMAN YOU STABBED IN THE ALLEY?
ONE OF MANY VICTIMS... BELIEVE IT OR NOT, I FREED HER.
WHERE IS THIS GATEWAY?
IT'S IN THE BASEMENT OF ST. PETER'S CATHEDRAL.
CAN IT BE SHUT DOWN?
IF IT CAN, I HAVE NO IDEA HOW. FOR NOW, THE BASEMENT IS SEALED, BUT EVIL SPIRITS KEEP SLIPPING THROUGH.
I REALLY SHOULD BE GETTING BACK. MAY I PLEASE HAVE THE KNIFE?
HERE YOU GO.

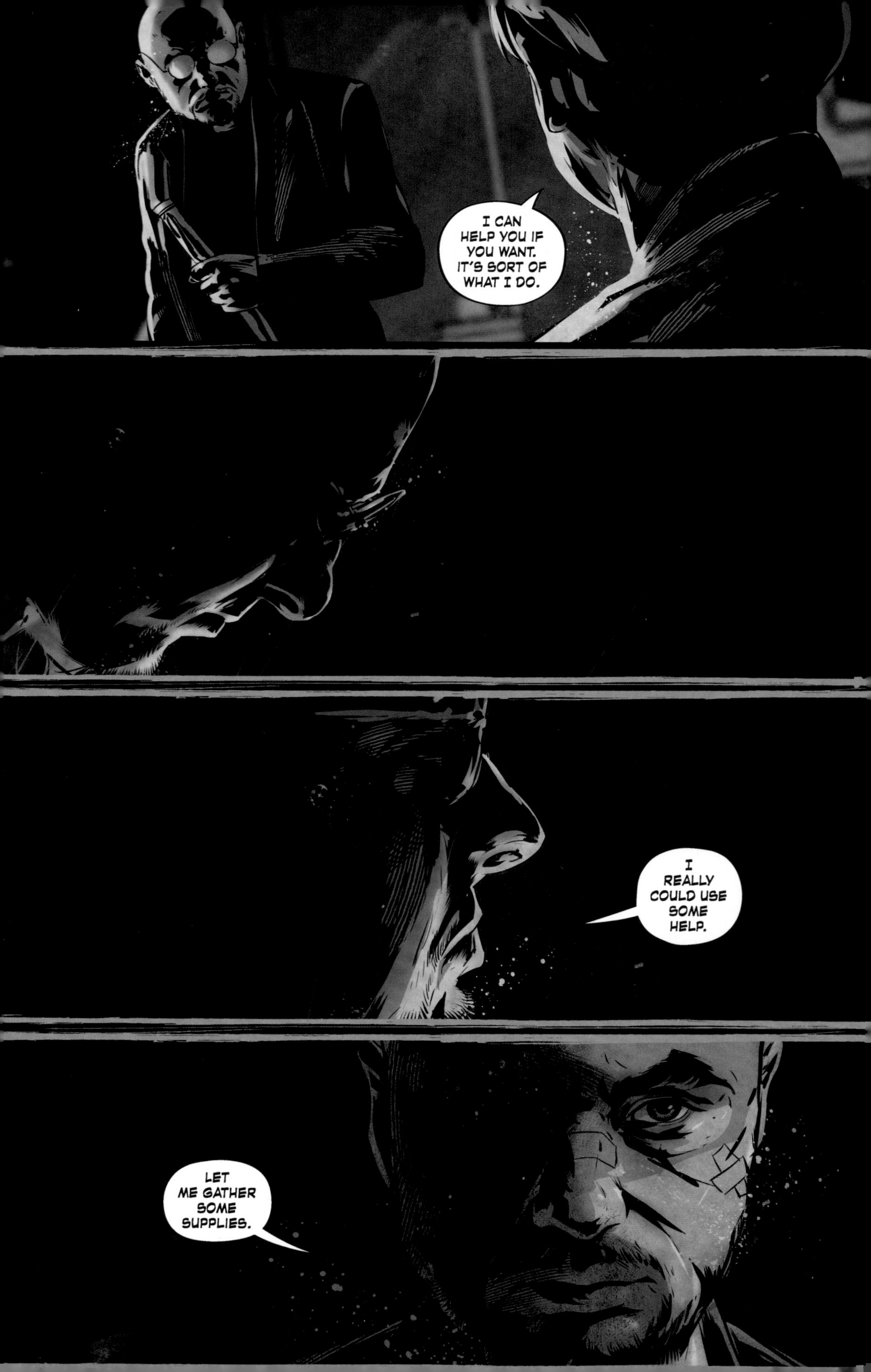
I CAN HELP YOU IF YOU WANT. IT'S SORT OF WHAT I DO.
I REALLY COULD USE SOME HELP.
LET ME GATHER SOME SUPPLIES.

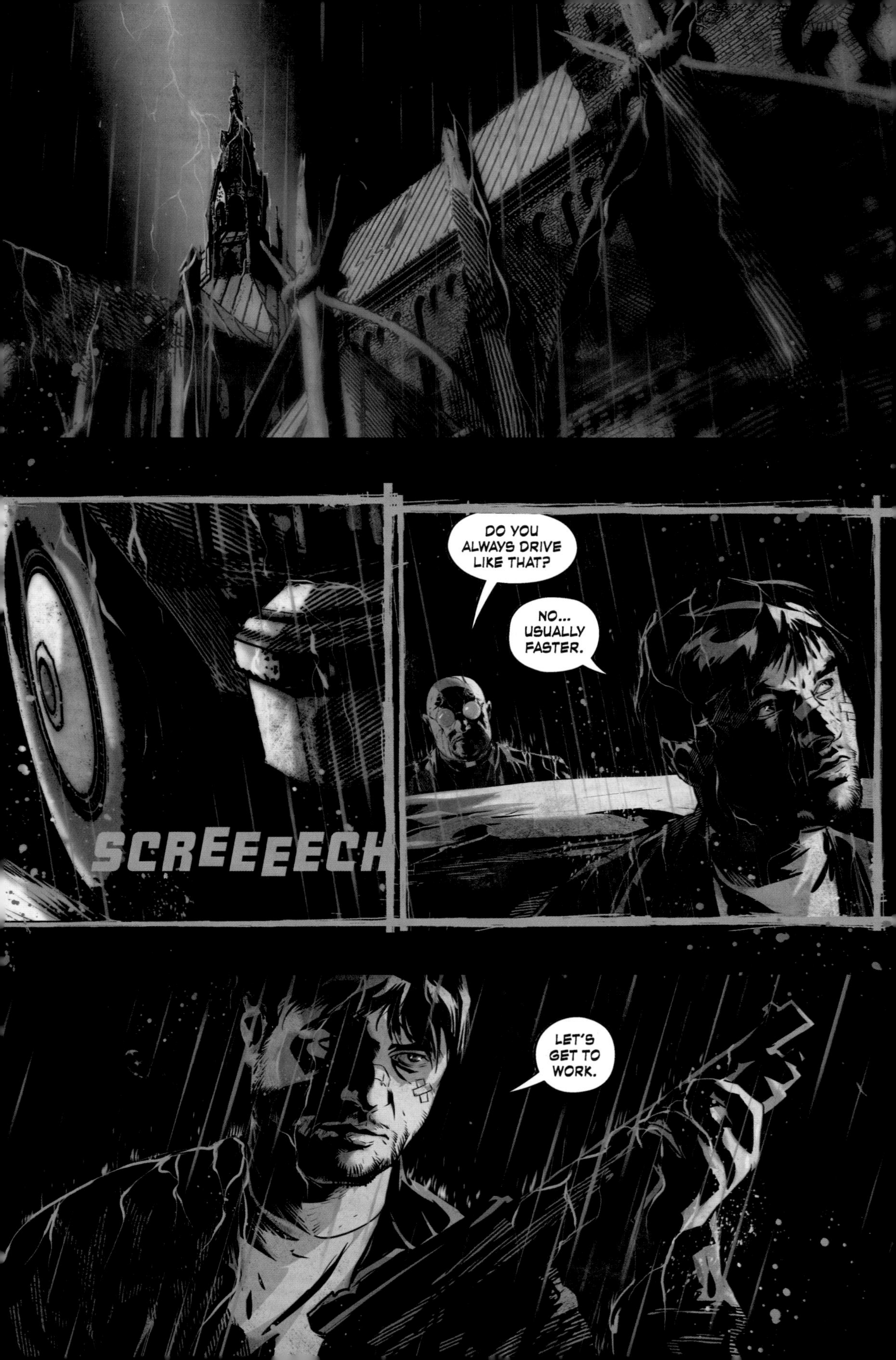
SCREEEECH
DO YOU ALWAYS DRIVE LIKE THAT?
NO... USUALLY FASTER.
LET'S GET TO WORK.

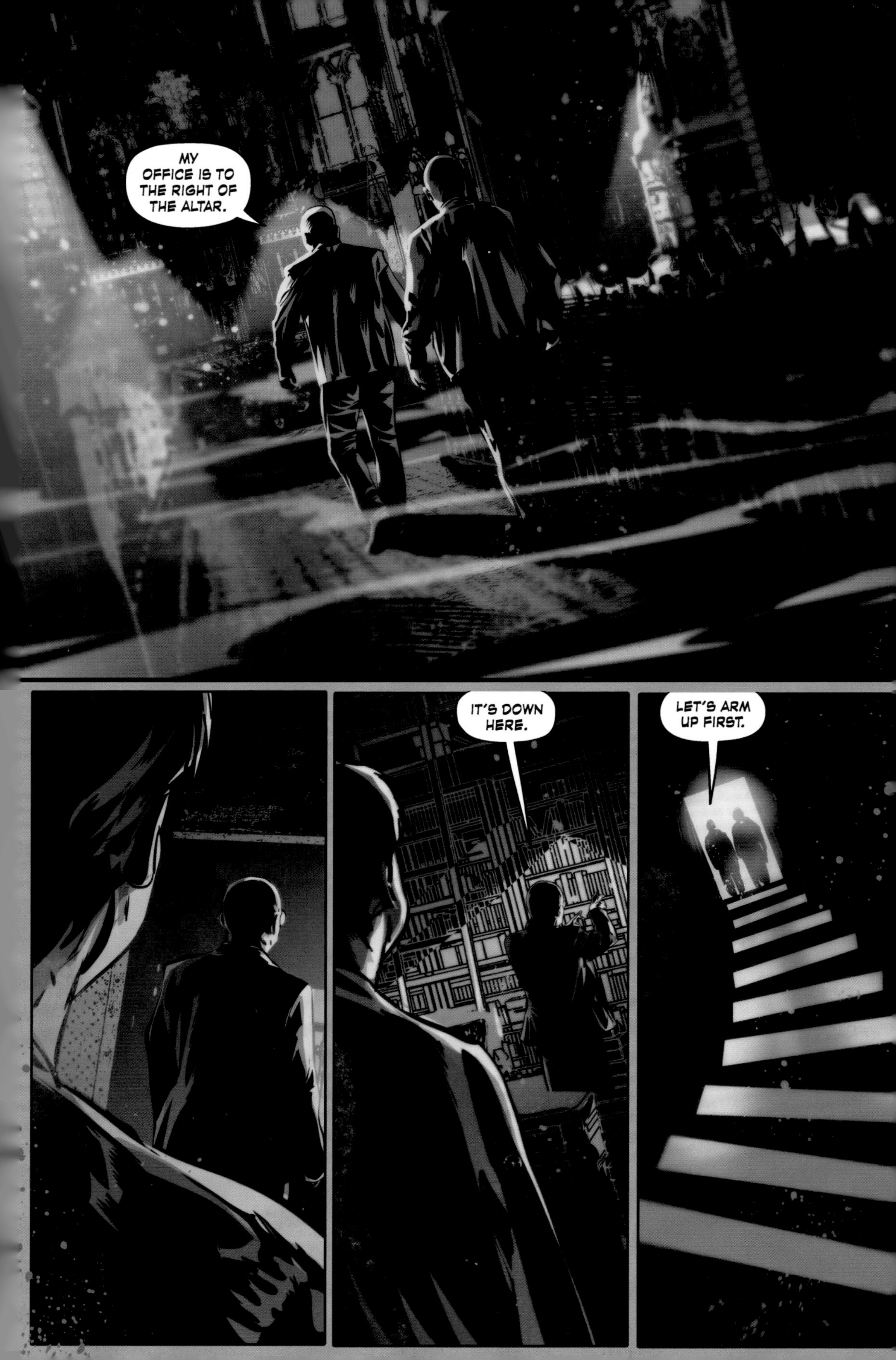
MY OFFICE IS TO THE RIGHT OF THE ALTAR.
IT'S DOWN HERE.
LET'S ARM UP FIRST.

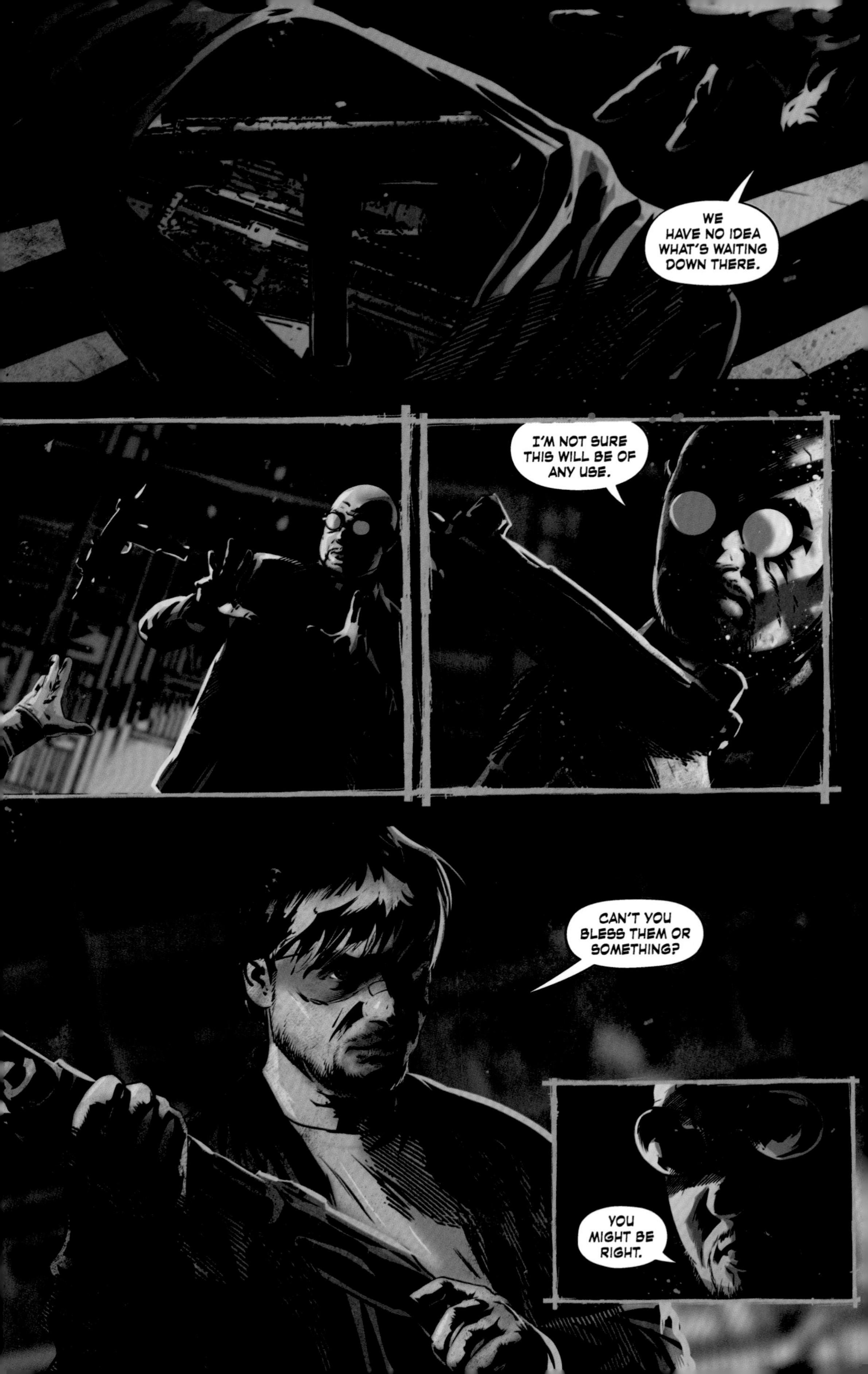
WE HAVE NO IDEA WHAT'S WAITING DOWN THERE.
I'M NOT SURE THIS WILL BE OF ANY USE.
CAN'T YOU BLESS THEM OR SOMETHING?
YOU MIGHT BE RIGHT.

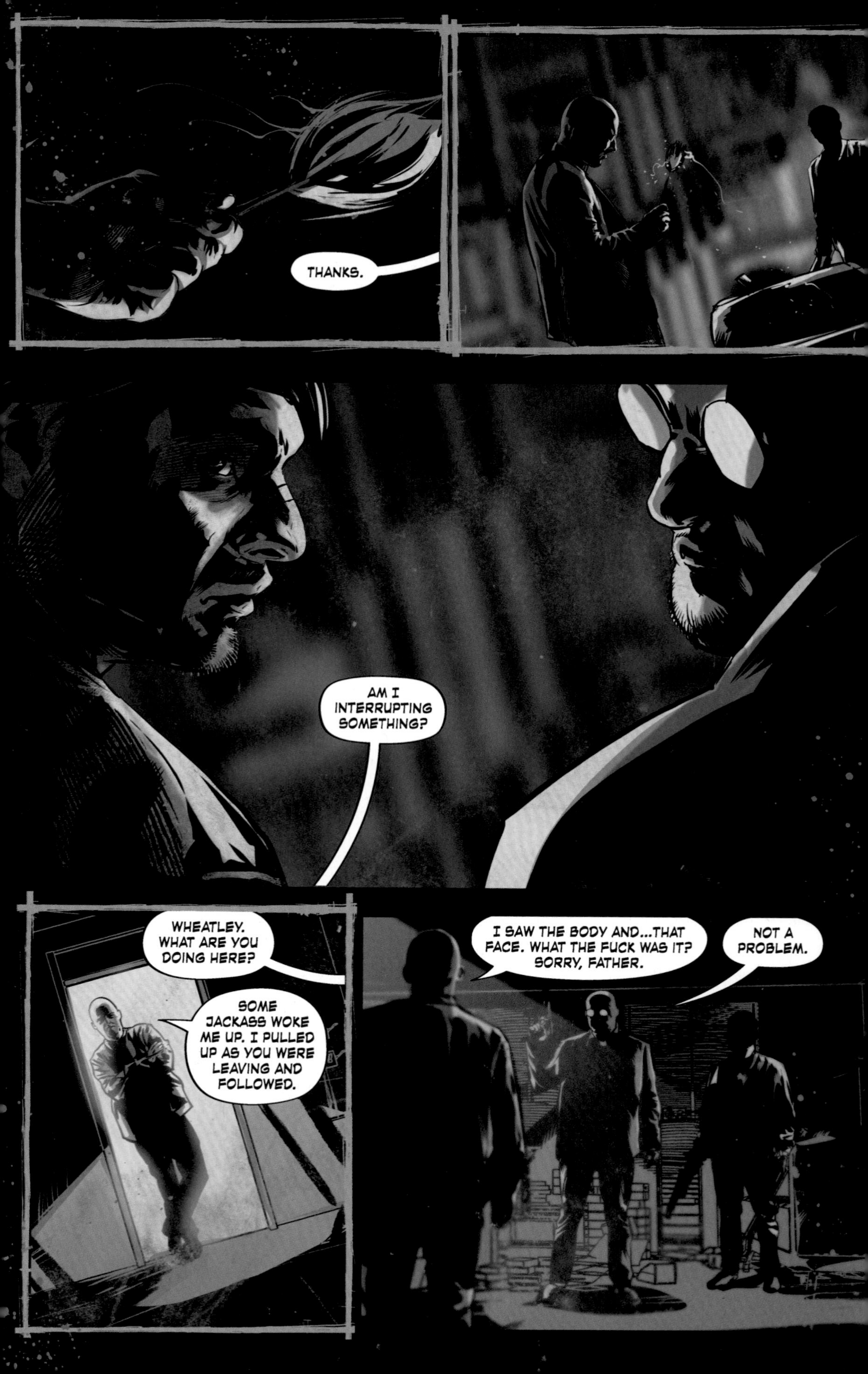
THANKS.
AM I INTERRUPTING SOMETHING?
WHEATLEY. WHAT ARE YOU DOING HERE?
SOME JACKASS WOKE ME UP. I PULLED UP AS YOU WERE LEAVING AND FOLLOWED.
I SAW THE BODY AND...THAT FACE. WHAT THE FUCK WAS IT? SORRY, FATHER.
NOT A PROBLEM.

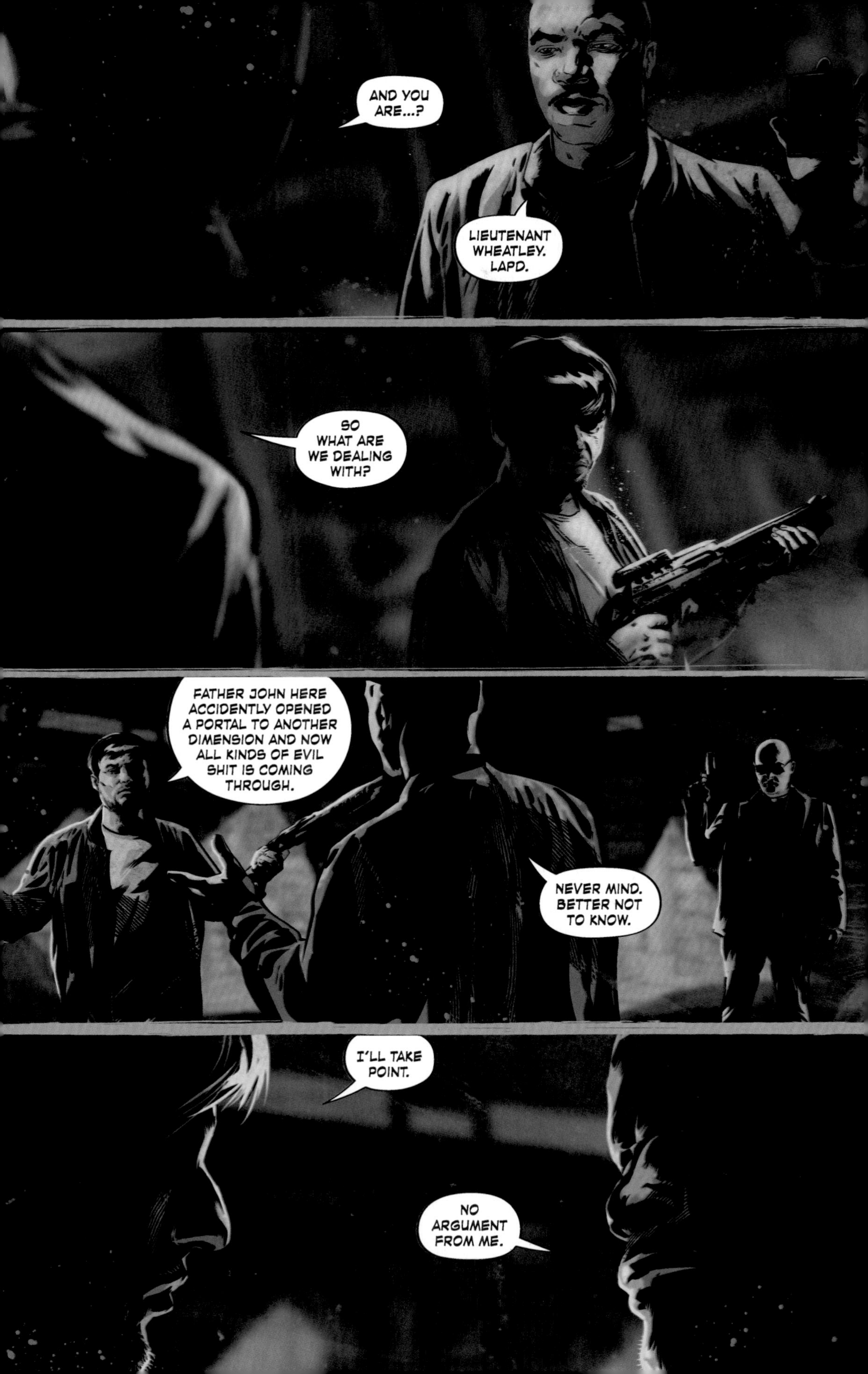
AND YOU ARE...?
LIEUTENANT WHEATLEY. LAPD.
SO WHAT ARE WE DEALING WITH?
FATHER JOHN HERE ACCIDENTLY OPENED A PORTAL TO ANOTHER DIMENSION AND NOW ALL KINDS OF EVIL SHIT IS COMING THROUGH.
NEVER MIND. BETTER NOT TO KNOW.
I'LL TAKE POINT.
NO ARGUMENT FROM ME.

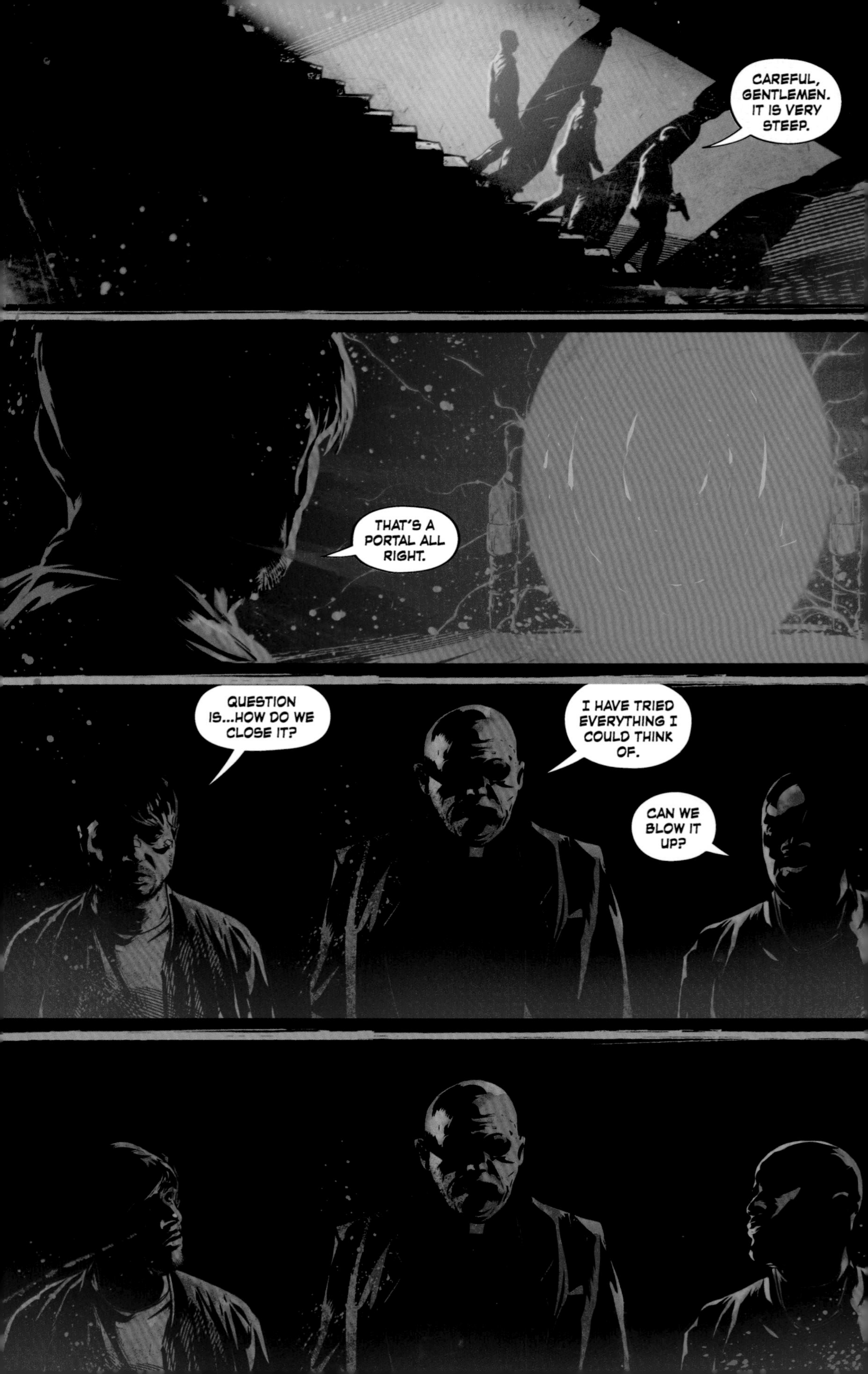
CAREFUL, GENTLEMEN. IT IS VERY STEEP.
THAT'S A PORTAL ALL RIGHT.
QUESTION IS...HOW DO WE CLOSE IT?
I HAVE TRIED EVERYTHING I COULD THINK OF.
CAN WE BLOW IT UP?

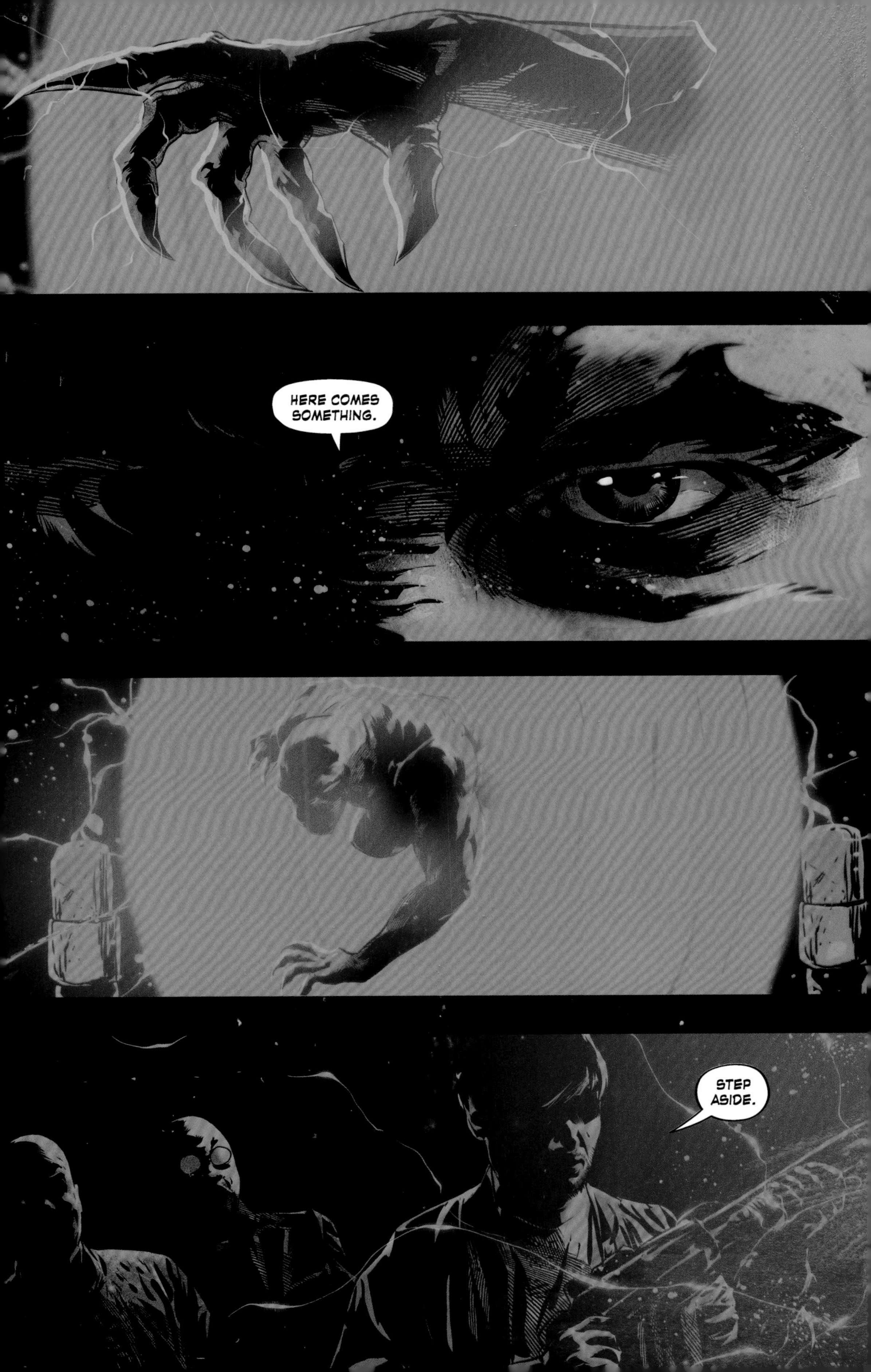
HERE COMES SOMETHING.
STEP ASIDE.

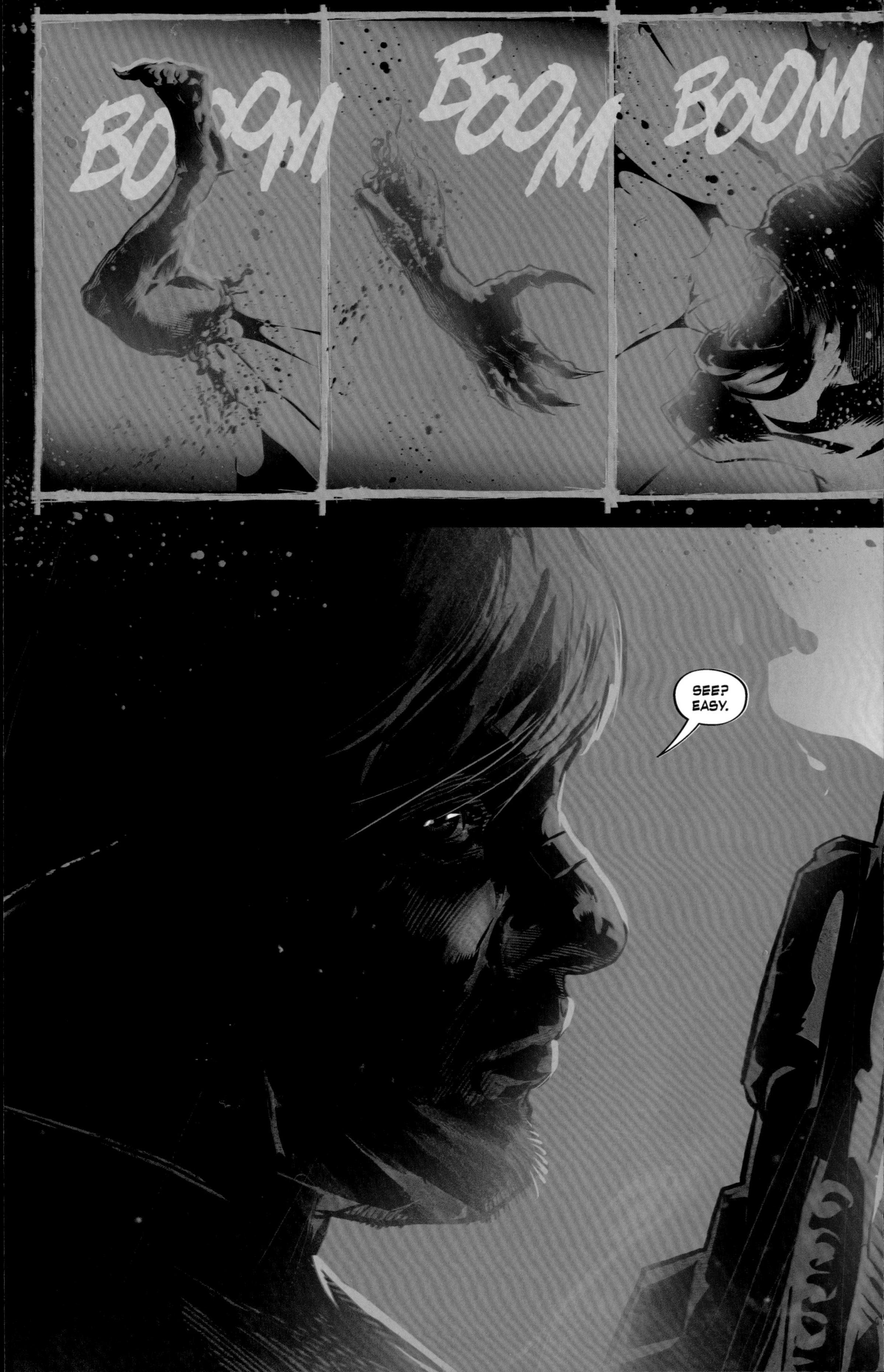
BOOM
BOOM
BOOM
SEE? EASY.

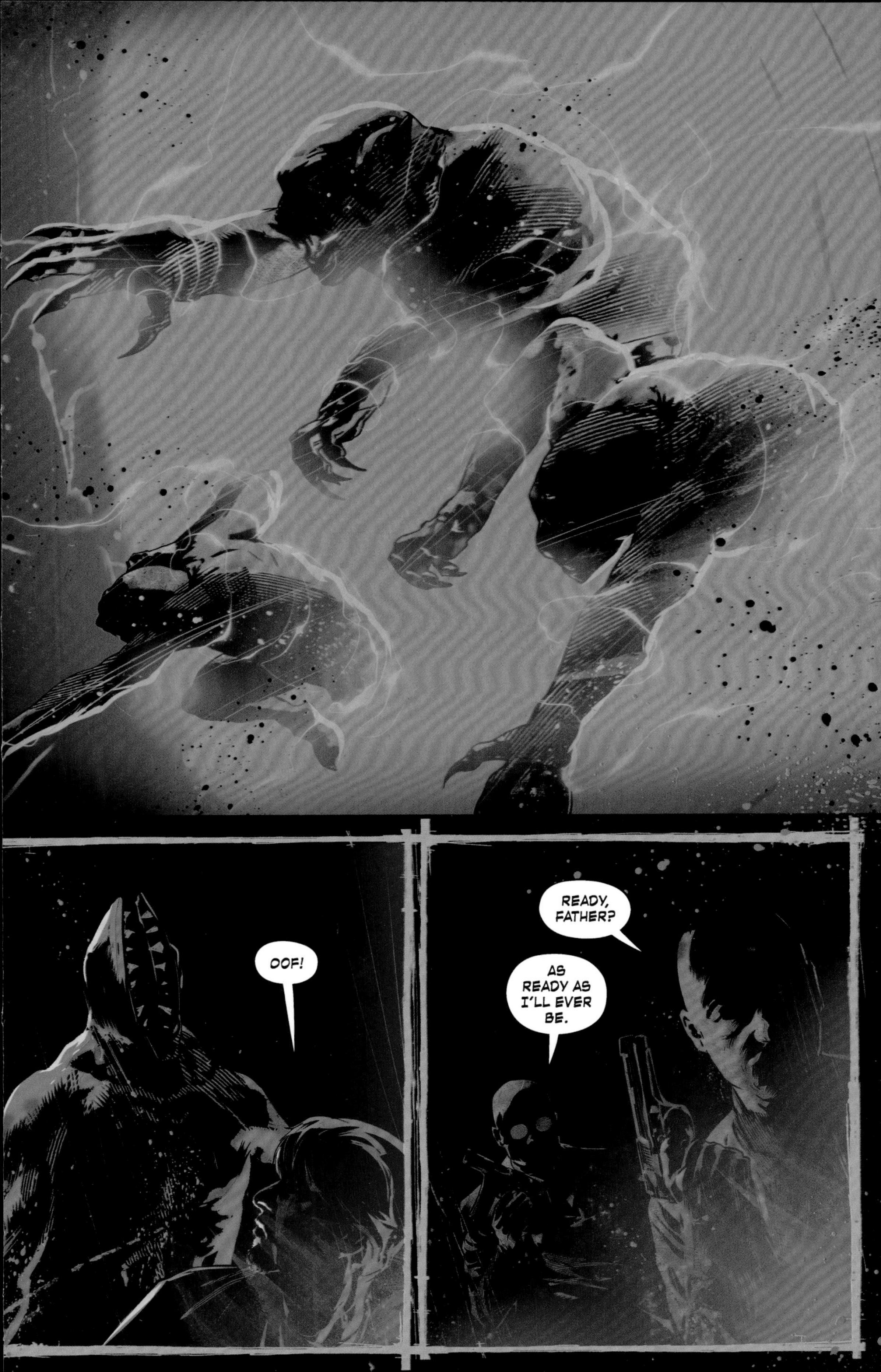
OOF!
READY, FATHER?
AS READY AS I'LL EVER BE.

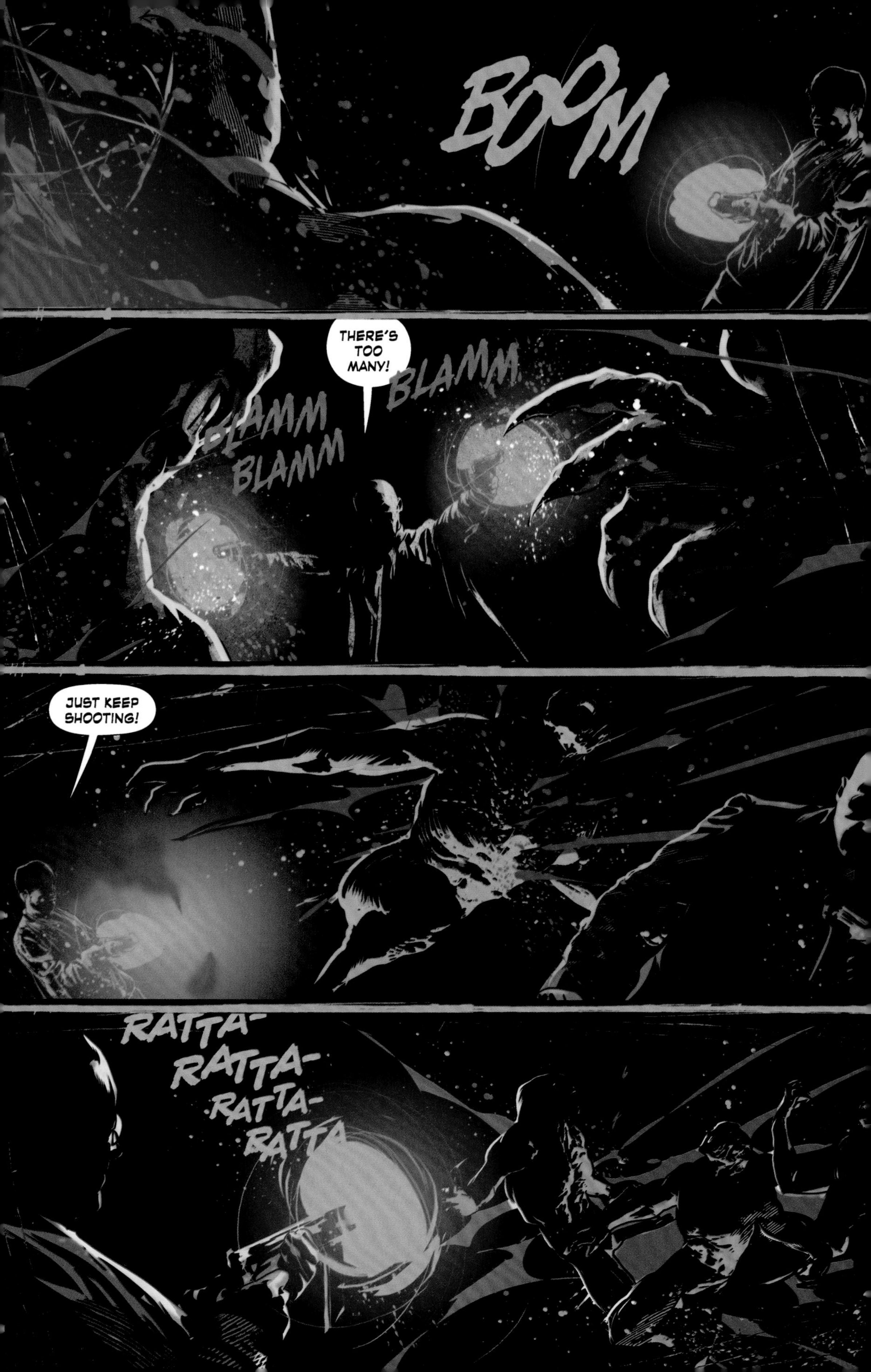
BOOM
THERE'S TOO MANY!
BLAMM
BLAMM
BLAMM
JUST KEEP SHOOTING!
RATTA-
RATTA-
RATTA-
RATTA

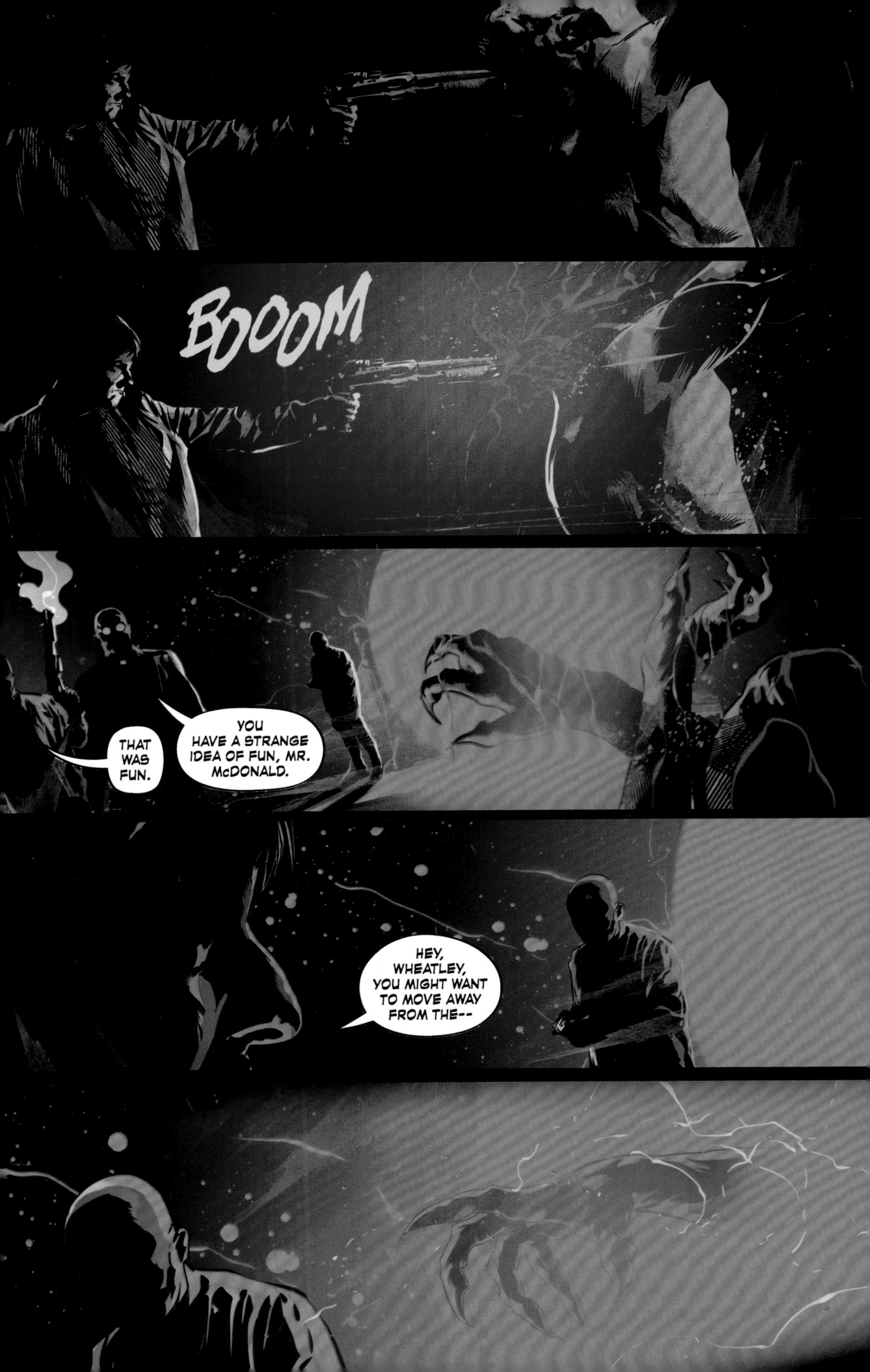
BOOOM
THAT WAS FUN.
YOU HAVE A STRANGE IDEA OF FUN, MR. McDONALD.
HEY, WHEATLEY, YOU MIGHT WANT TO MOVE AWAY FROM THE--

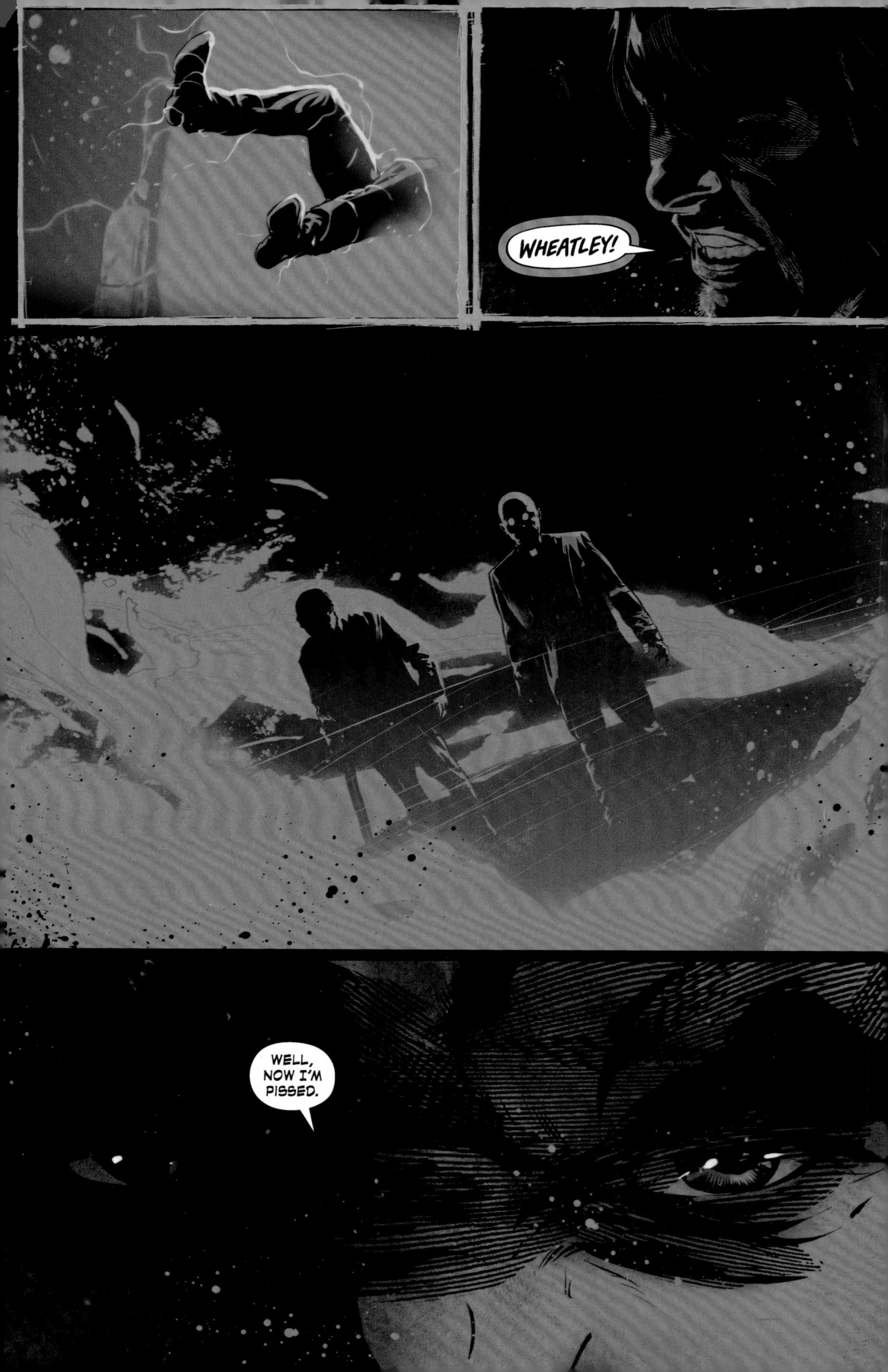
WHEATLEY!
WELL, NOW I'M PISSED.

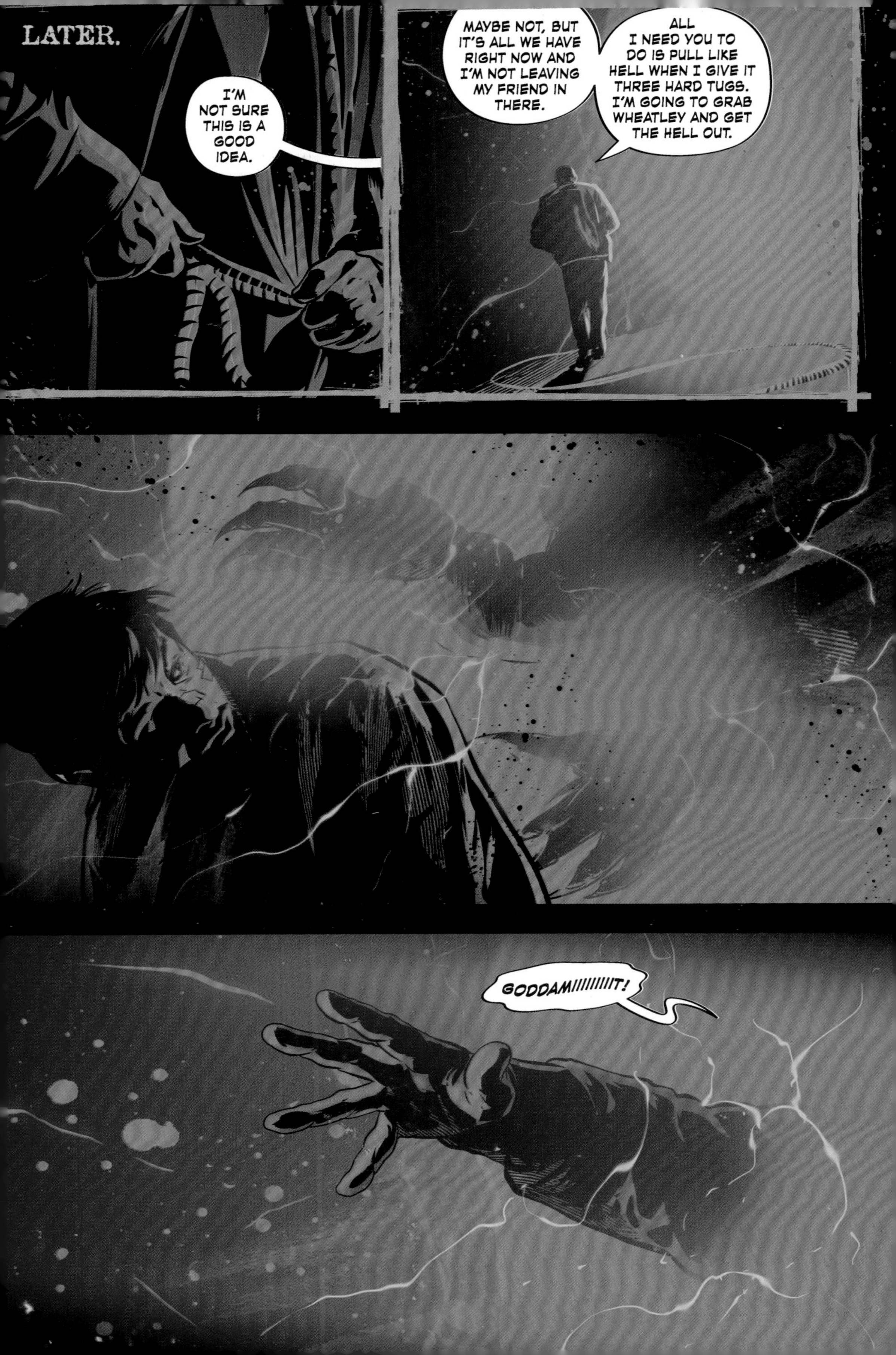
LATER.
I'M NOT SURE THIS IS A GOOD IDEA.
MAYBE NOT, BUT IT'S ALL WE HAVE RIGHT NOW AND I'M NOT LEAVING MY FRIEND IN THERE.
ALL I NEED YOU TO DO IS PULL LIKE HELL WHEN I GIVE IT THREE HARD TUGS. I'M GOING TO GRAB WHEATLEY AND GET THE HELL OUT.
GODDAMIIIIIIIIIT!

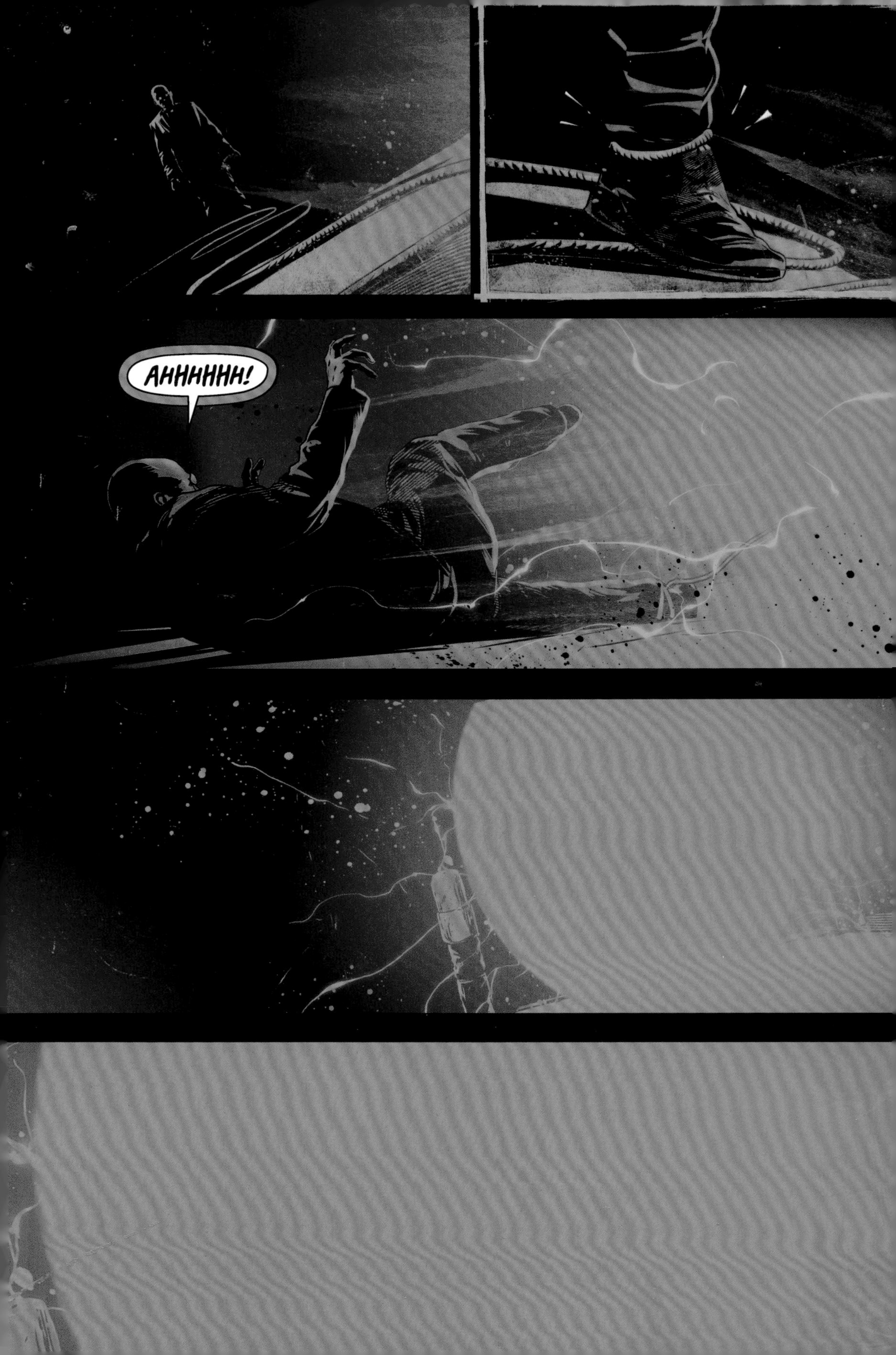
AHHHHHH!

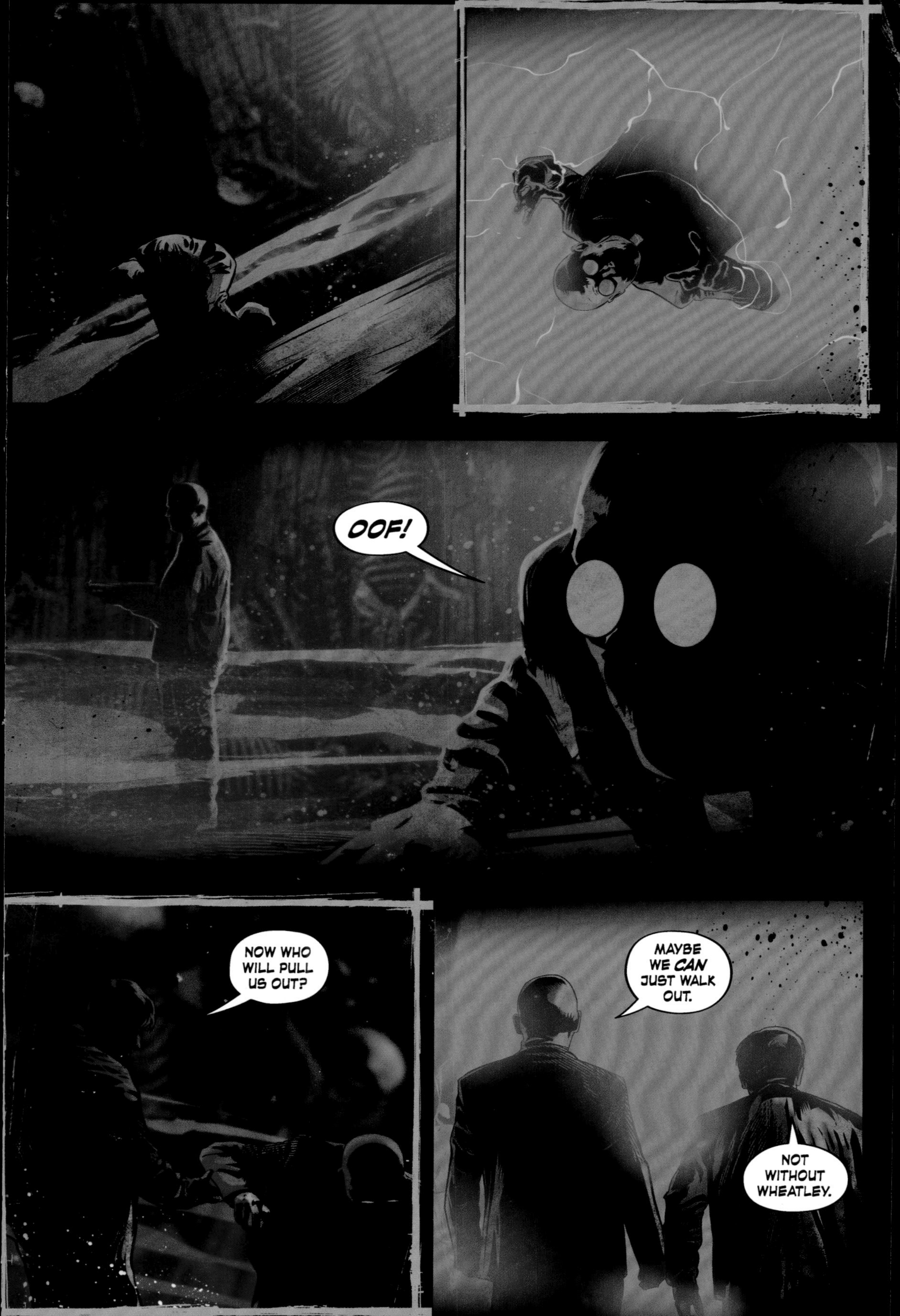
OOF!
NOW WHO WILL PULL US OUT?
MAYBE WE CAN JUST WALK OUT.
NOT WITHOUT WHEATLEY.

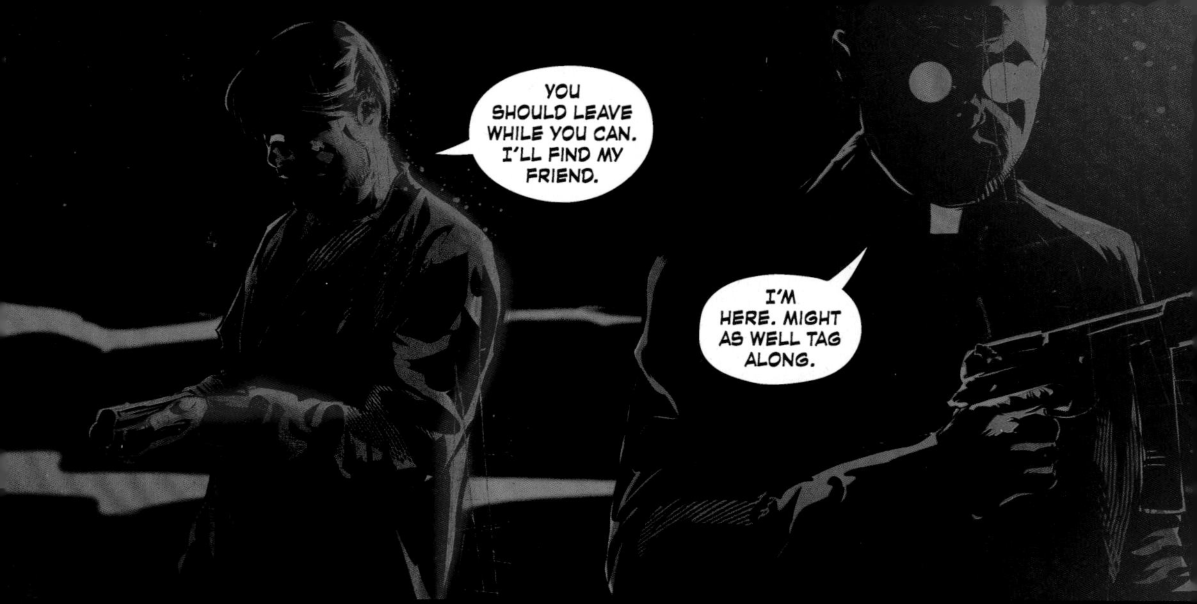
YOU SHOULD LEAVE WHILE YOU CAN. I'LL FIND MY FRIEND.
I'M HERE. MIGHT AS WELL TAG ALONG.

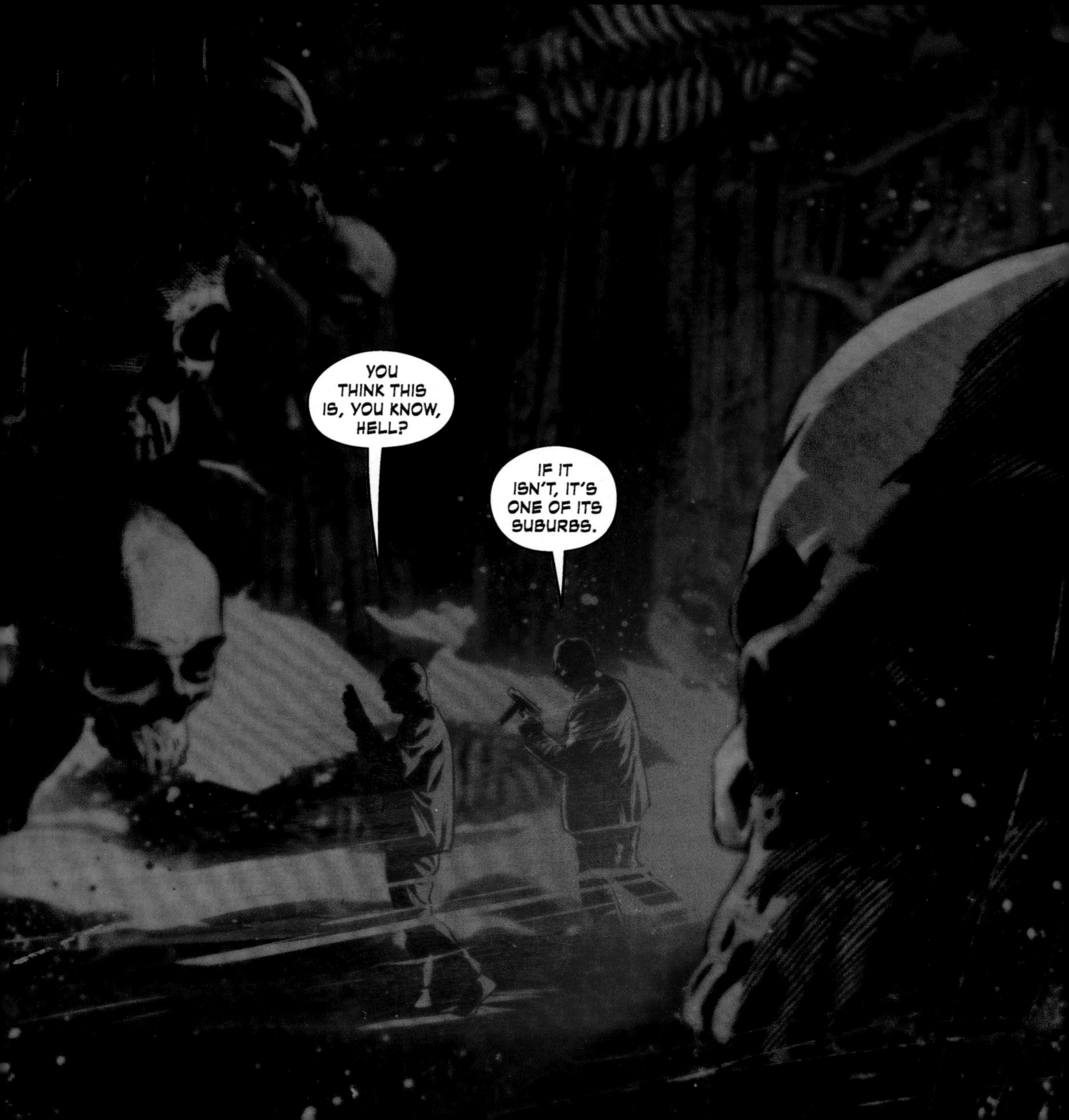
YOU THINK THIS IS, YOU KNOW, HELL?
IF IT ISN'T, IT'S ONE OF ITS SUBURBS.

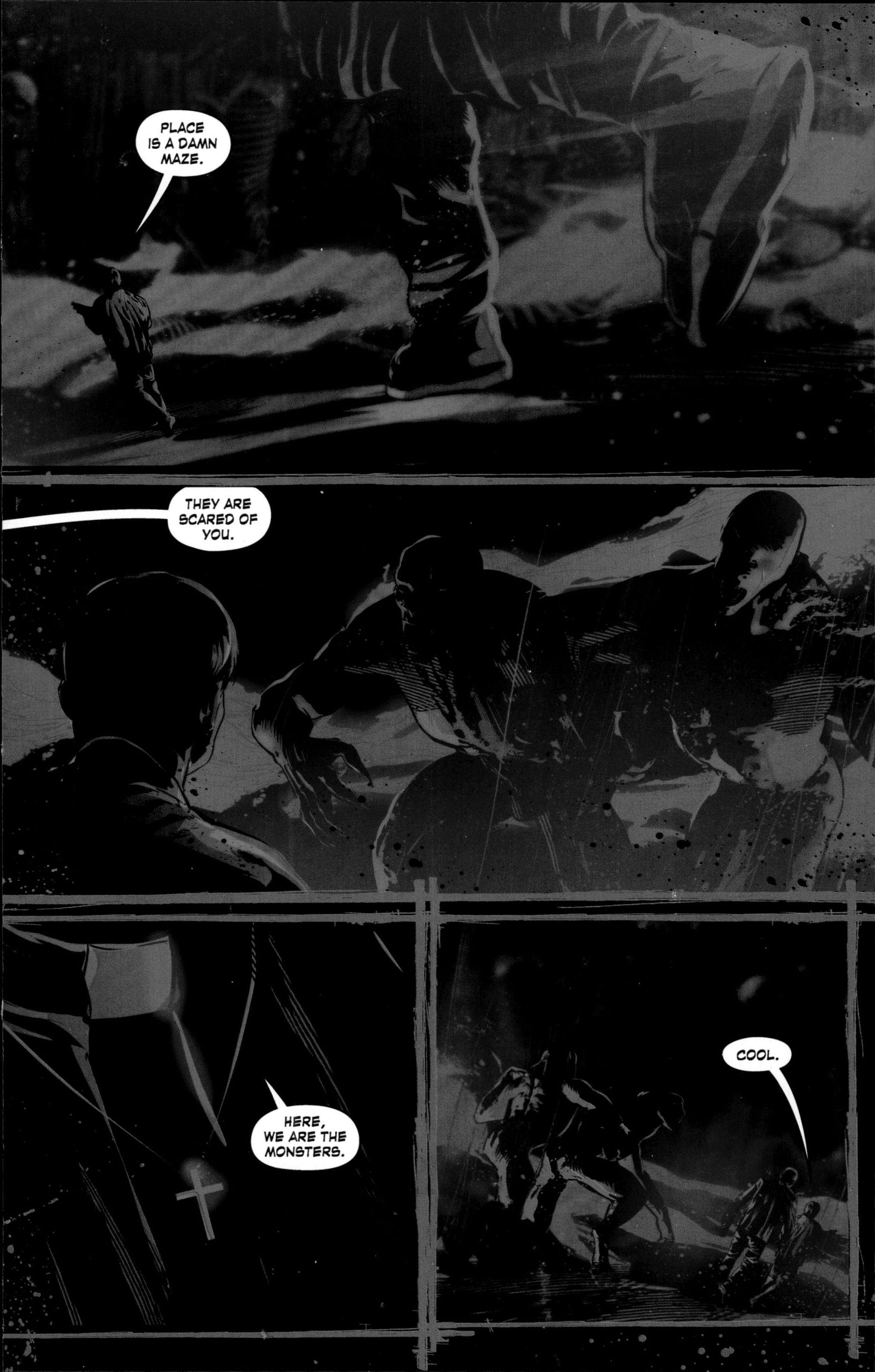
PLACE IS A DAMN MAZE.
THEY ARE SCARED OF YOU.
HERE, WE ARE THE MONSTERS.
COOL.

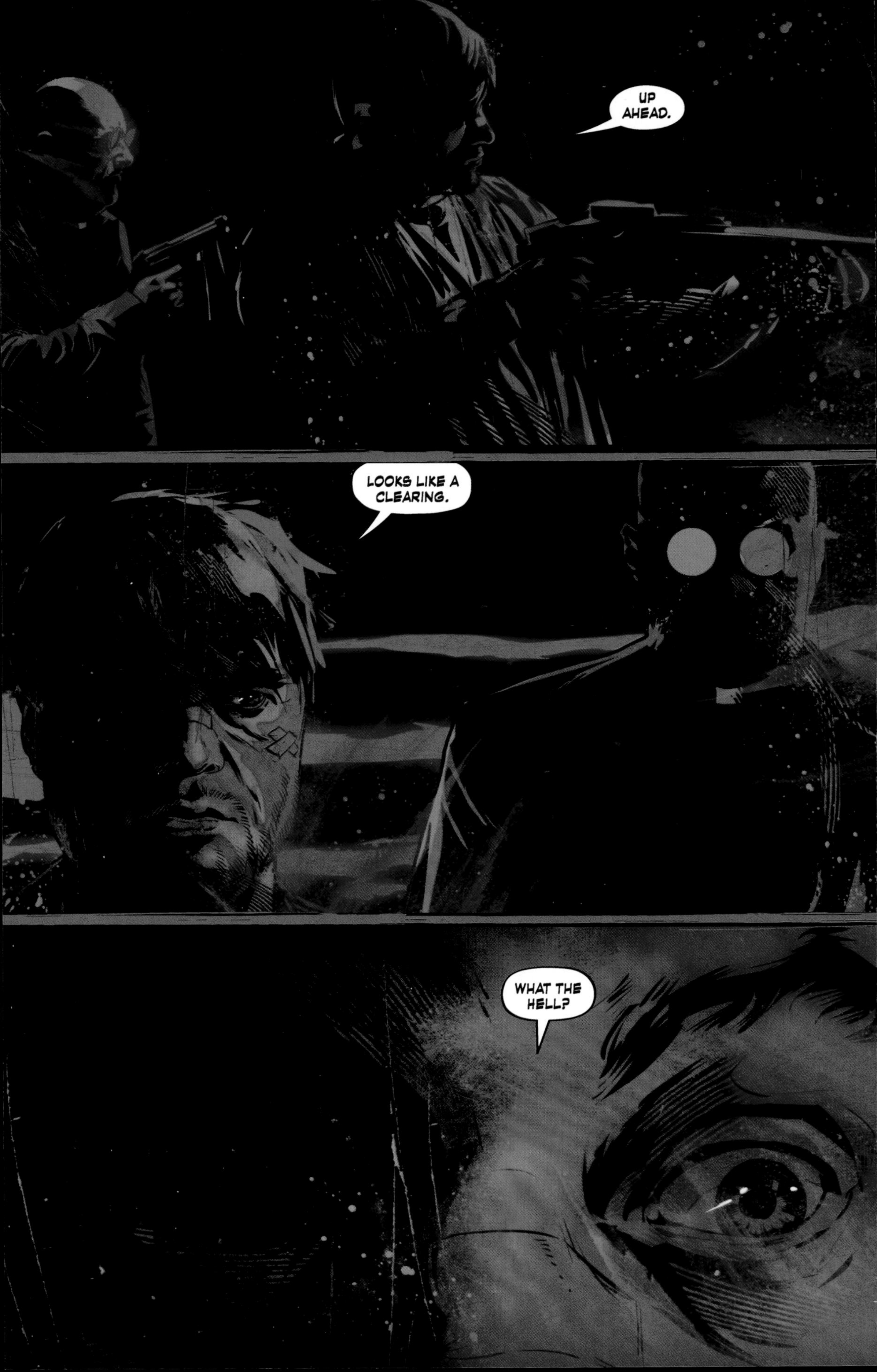
UP AHEAD.
LOOKS LIKE A CLEARING.
WHAT THE HELL?

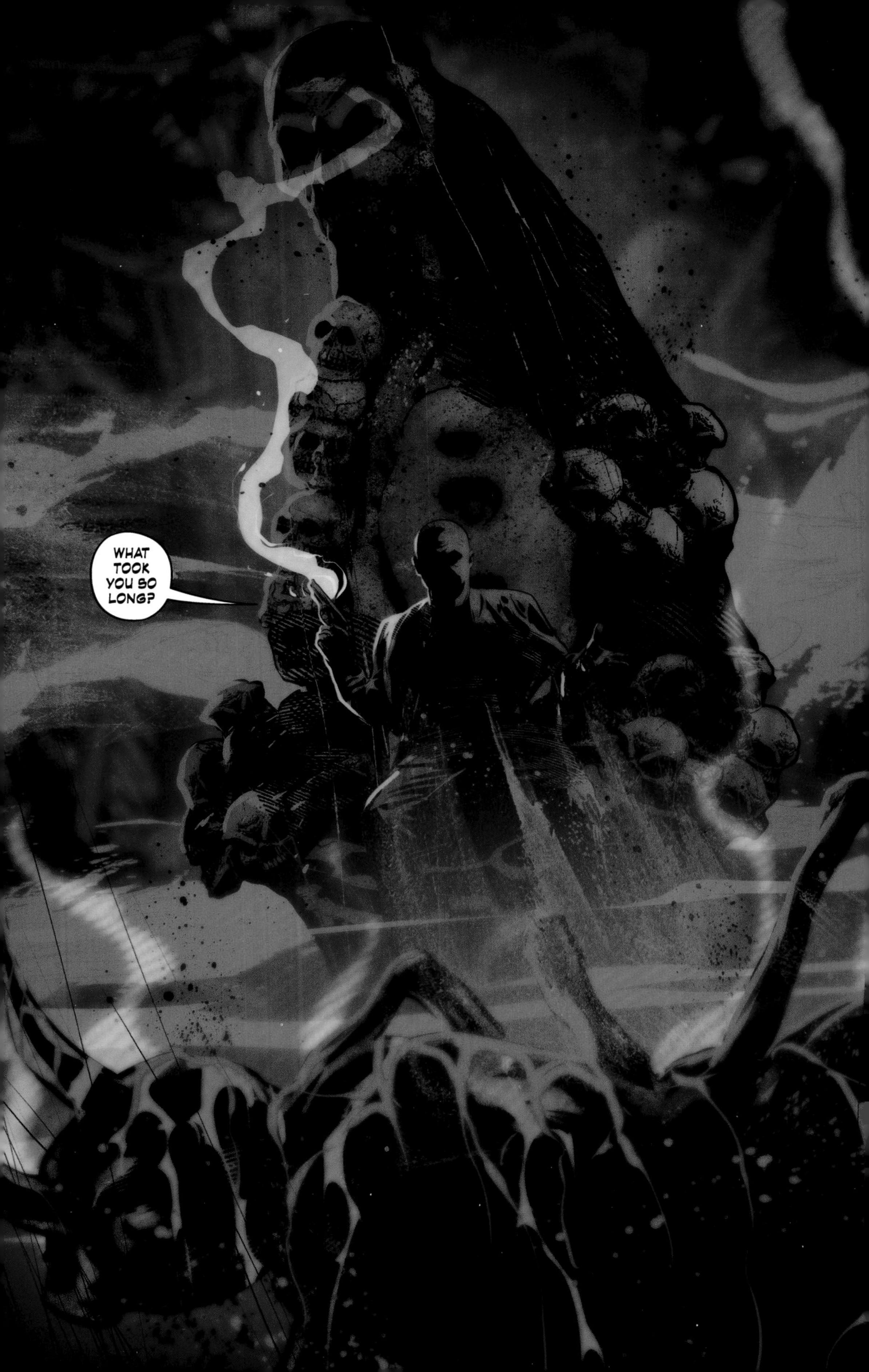
WHAT TOOK YOU SO LONG?

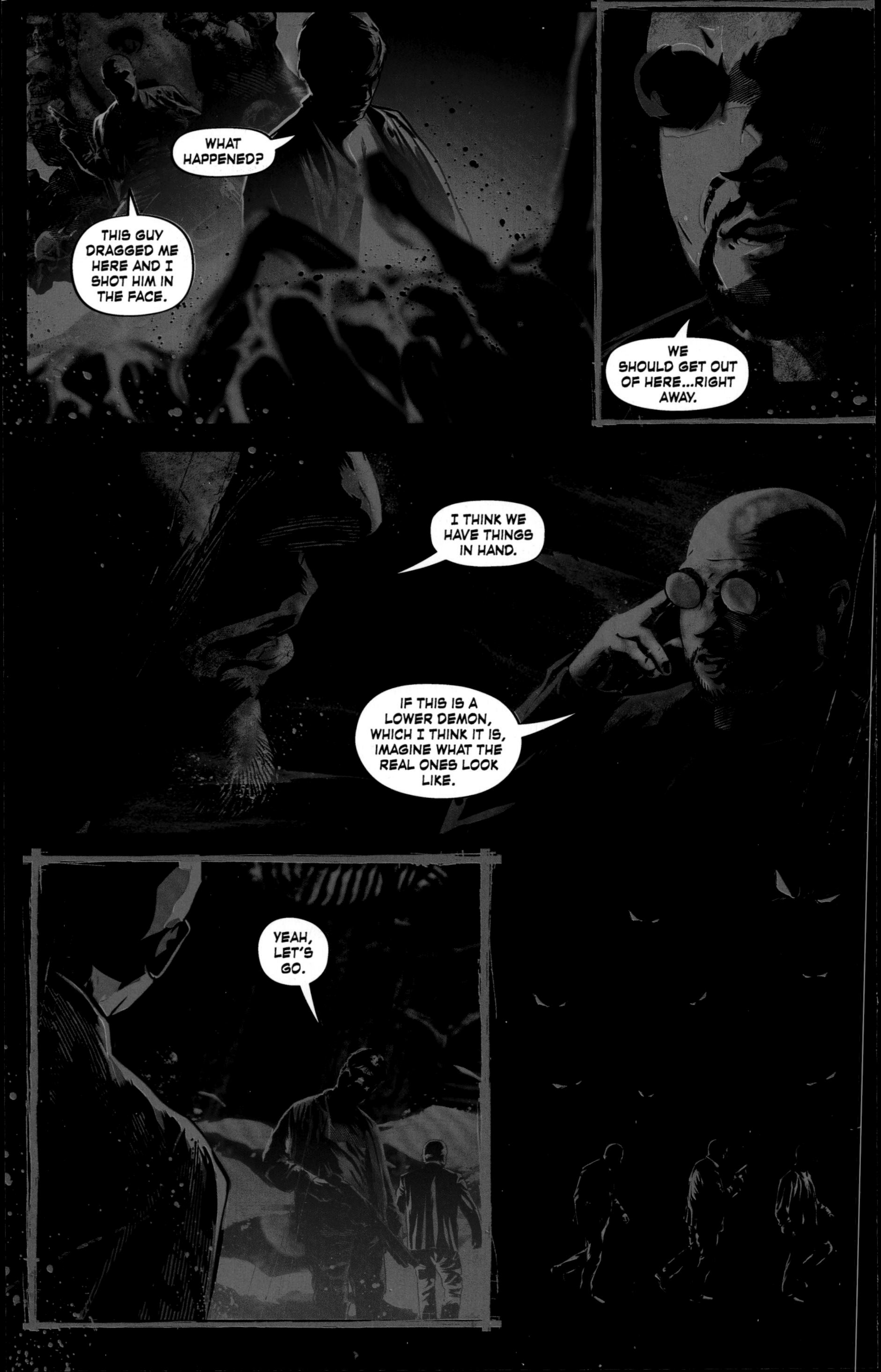
WHAT HAPPENED?
THIS GUY DRAGGED ME HERE AND I SHOT HIM IN THE FACE.
WE SHOULD GET OUT OF HERE...RIGHT AWAY.
I THINK WE HAVE THINGS IN HAND.
IF THIS IS A LOWER DEMON, WHICH I THINK IT IS, IMAGINE WHAT THE REAL ONES LOOK LIKE.
YEAH, LET'S GO.

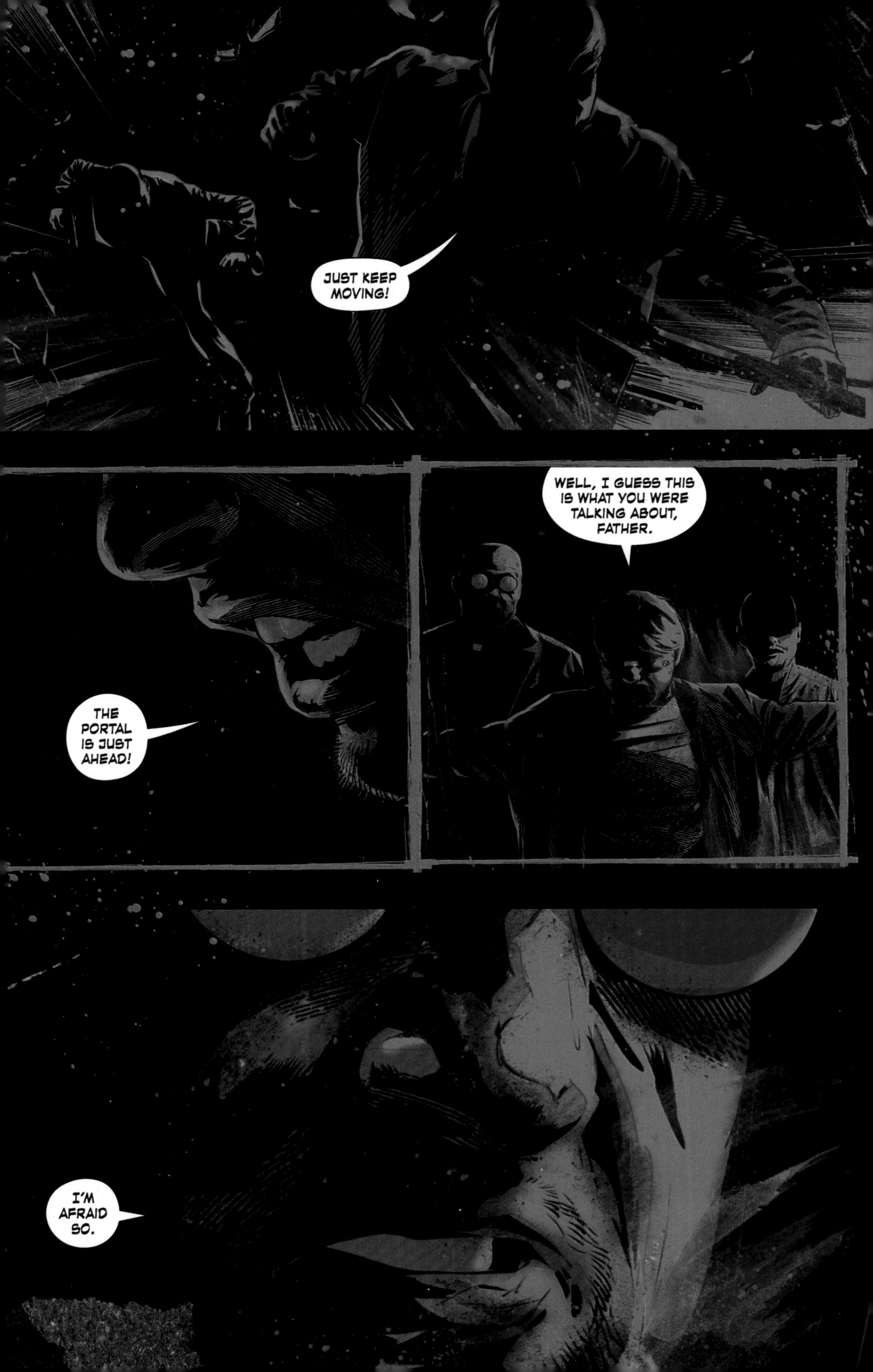
JUST KEEP MOVING!
THE PORTAL IS JUST AHEAD!
WELL, I GUESS THIS IS WHAT YOU WERE TALKING ABOUT, FATHER.
I'M AFRAID SO.

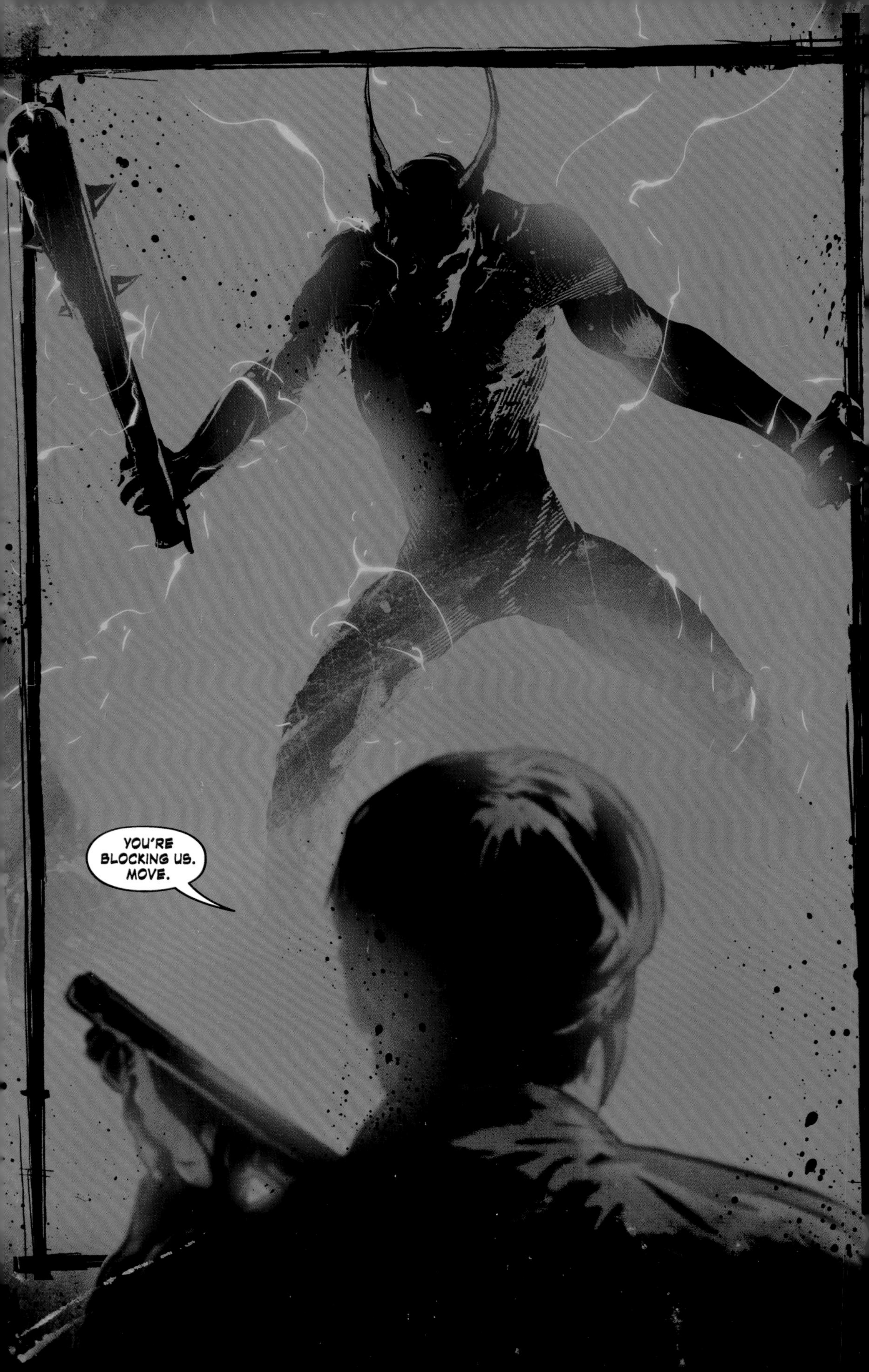
YOU'RE BLOCKING US. MOVE.

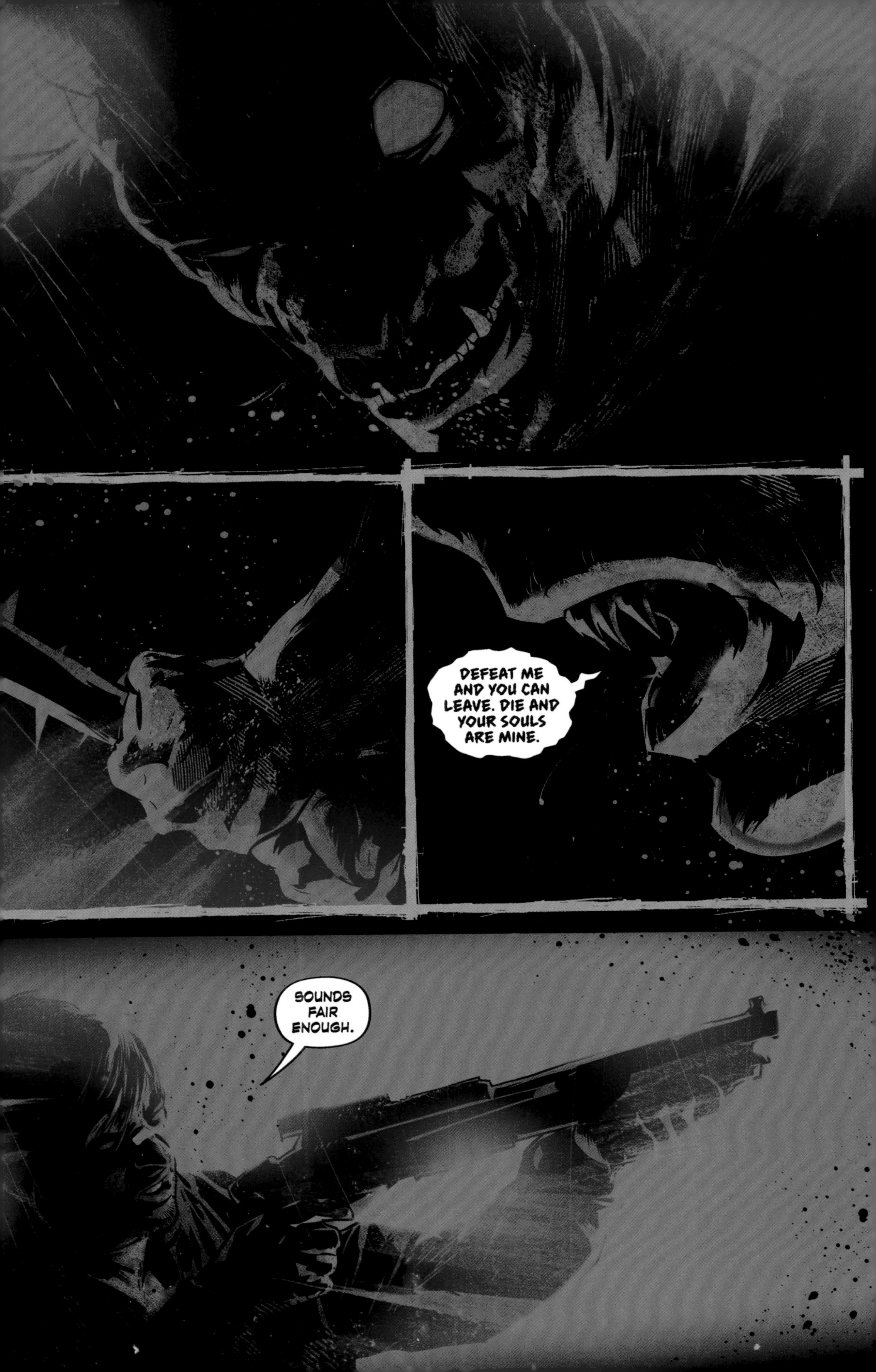
DEFEAT ME AND YOU CAN LEAVE. DIE AND YOUR SOULS ARE MINE.
SOUNDS FAIR ENOUGH.

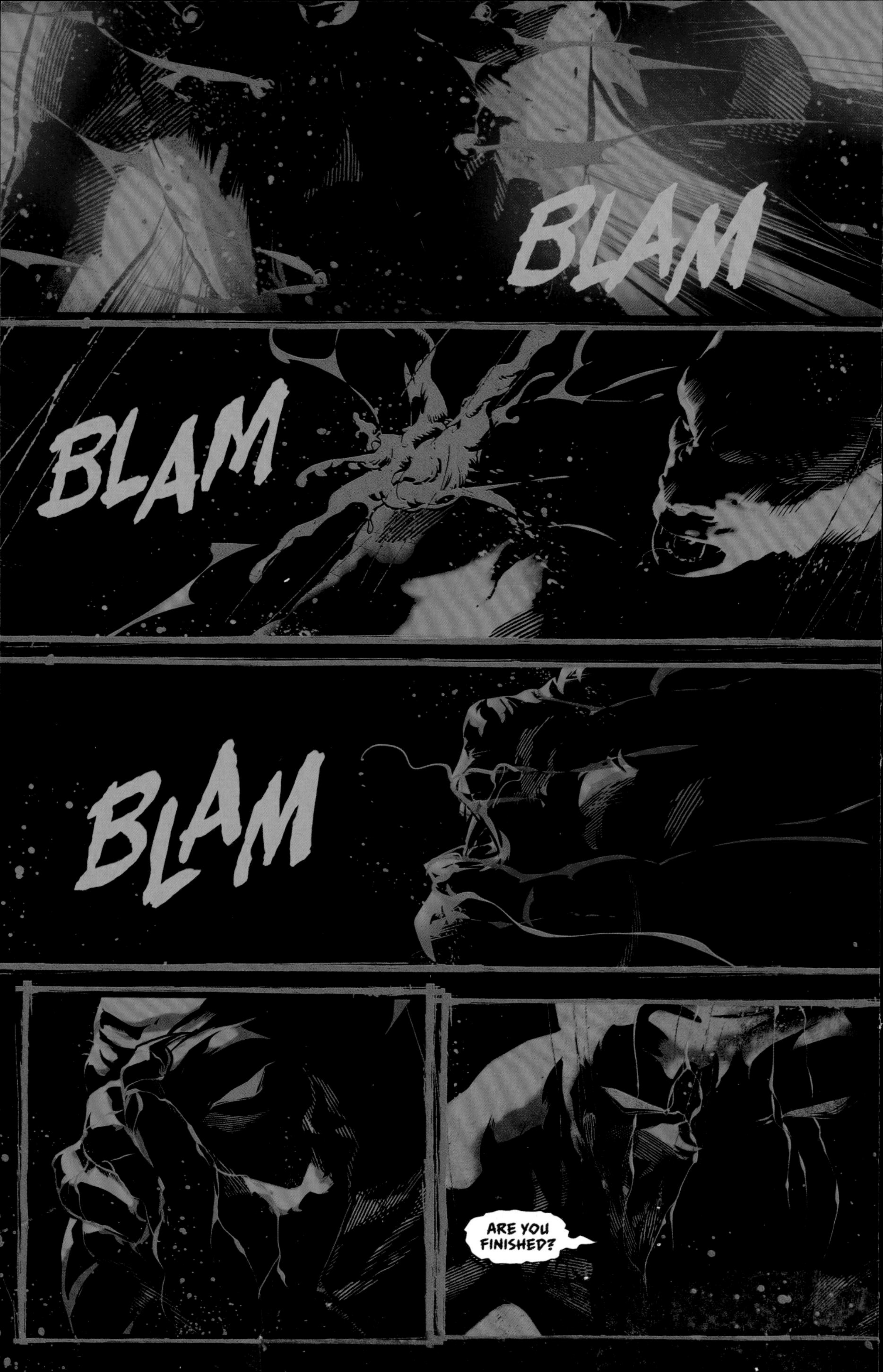
BLAM
BLAM
BLAM
ARE YOU FINISHED?

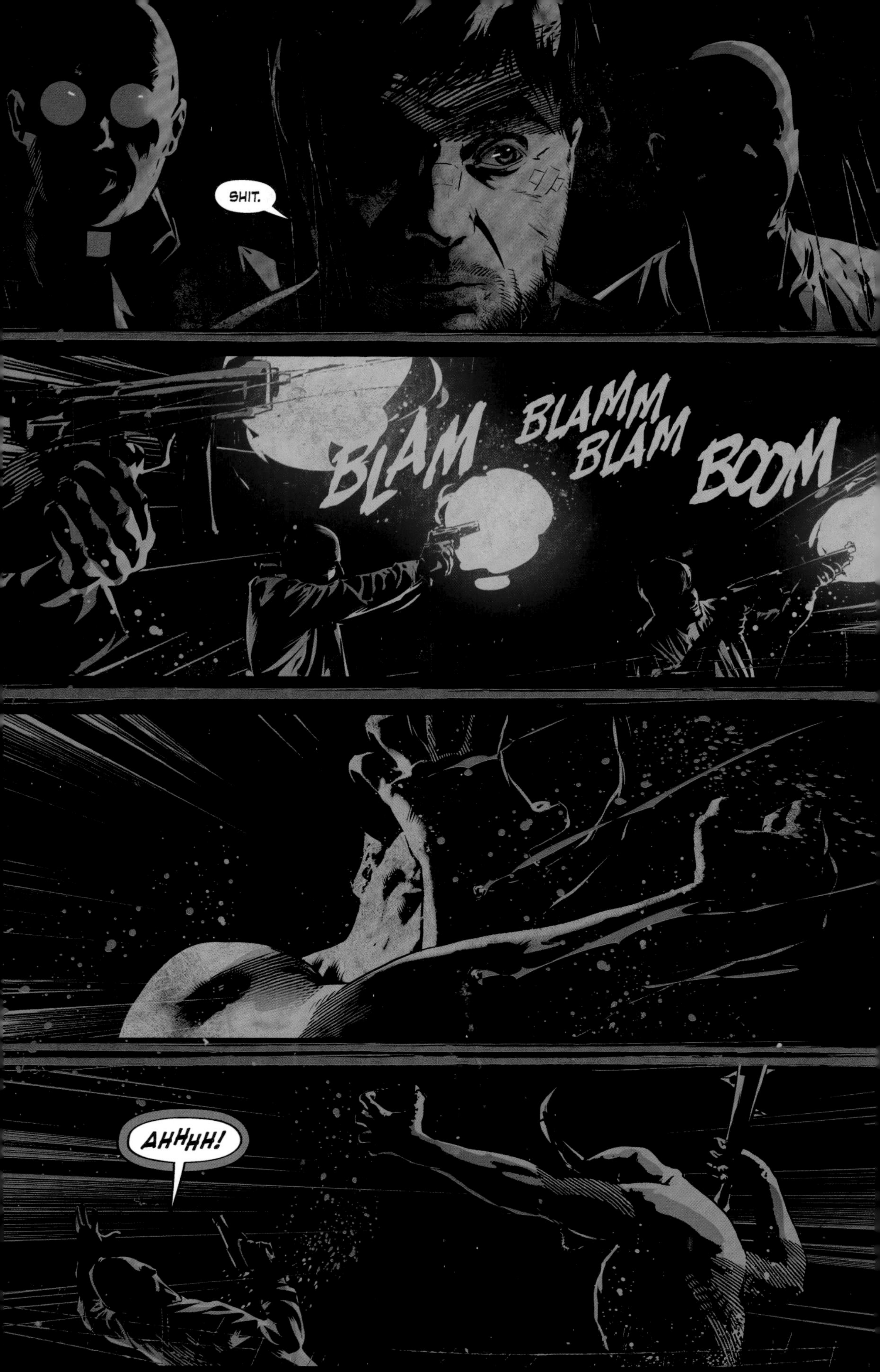
SHIT.
BLAM
BLAMM
BLAM
BOOM
AHHHH!

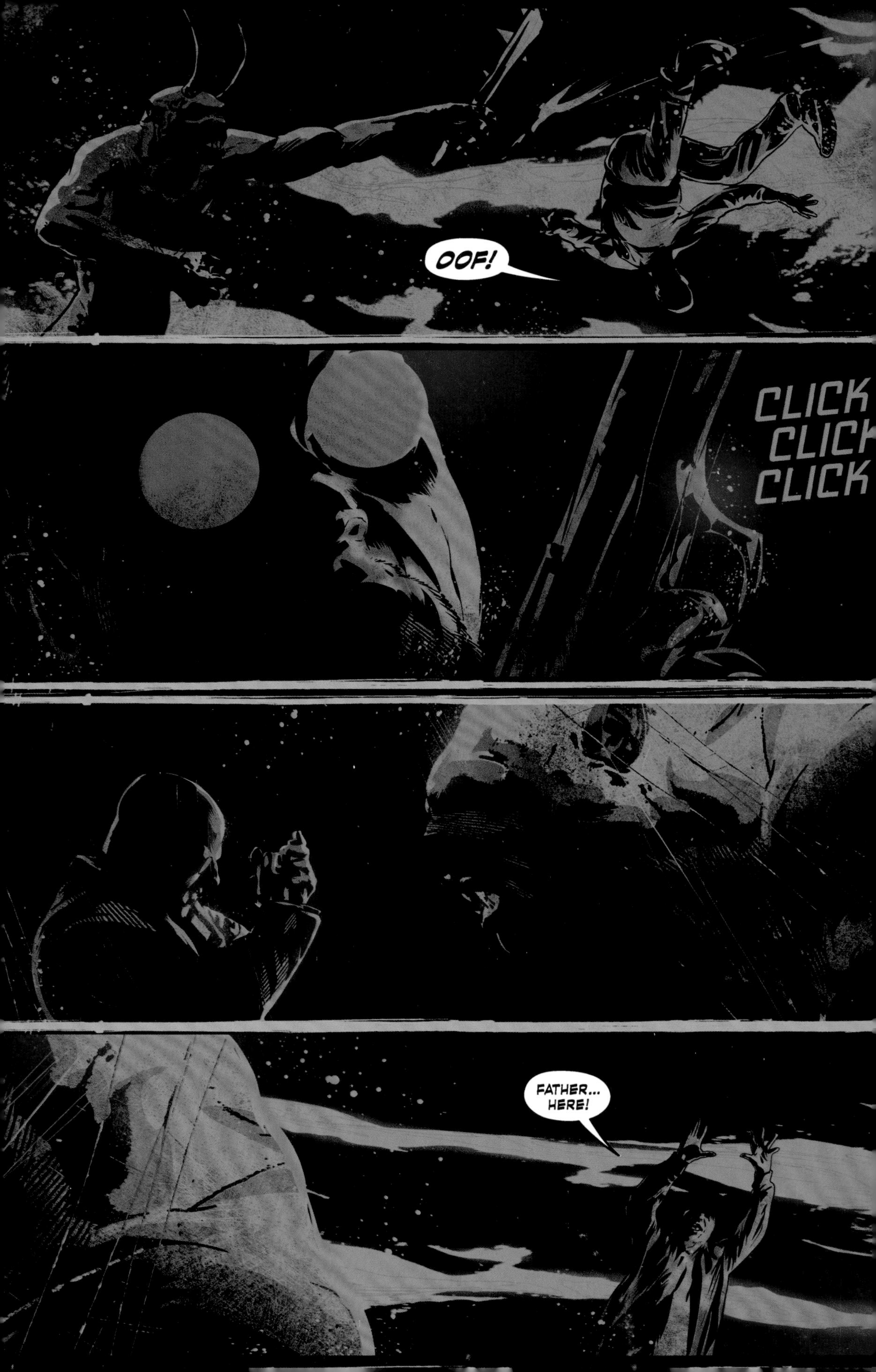
OOF!
CLICK
CLICK
CLICK
FATHER... HERE!

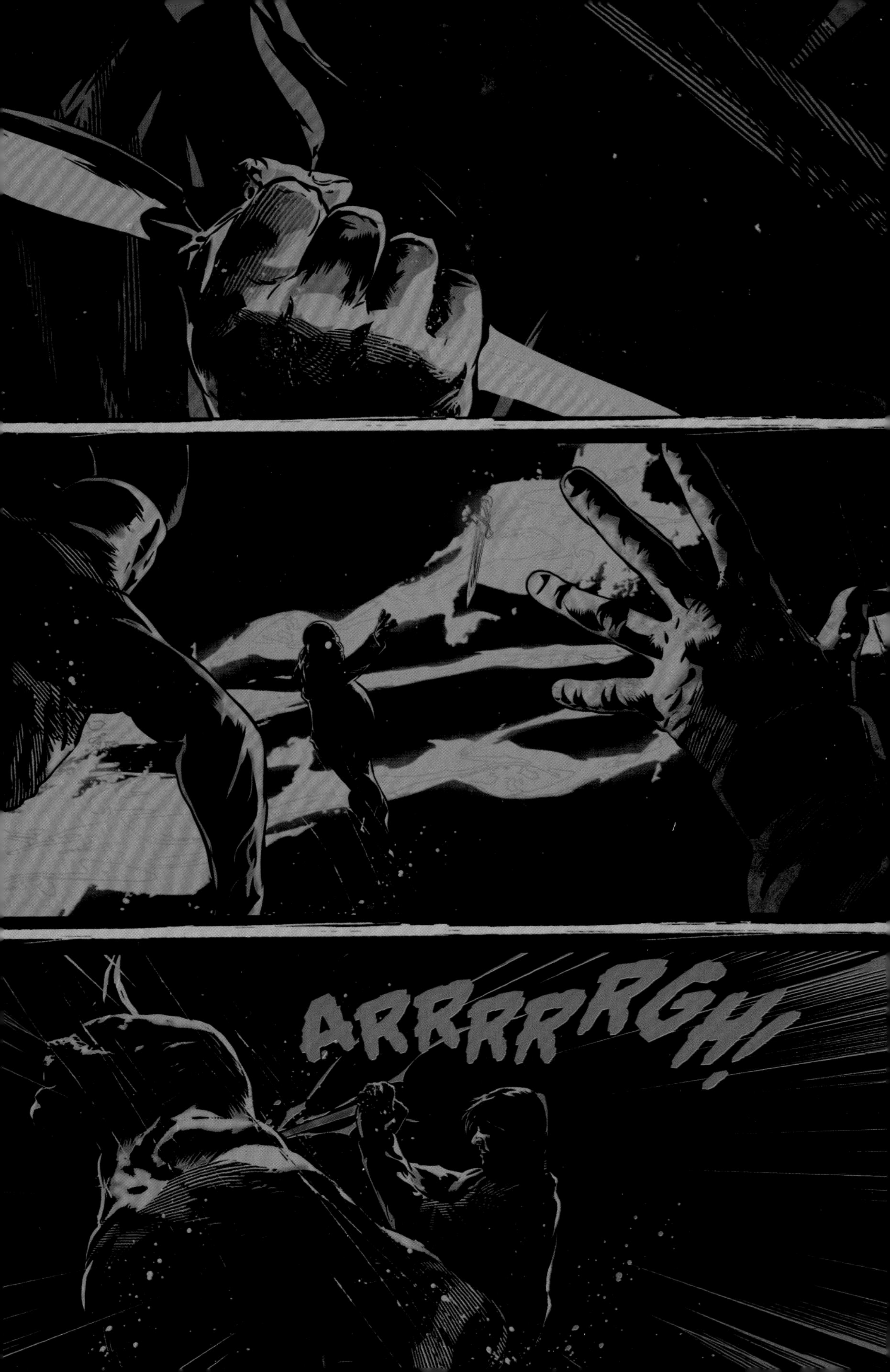
ARRRRRGH!

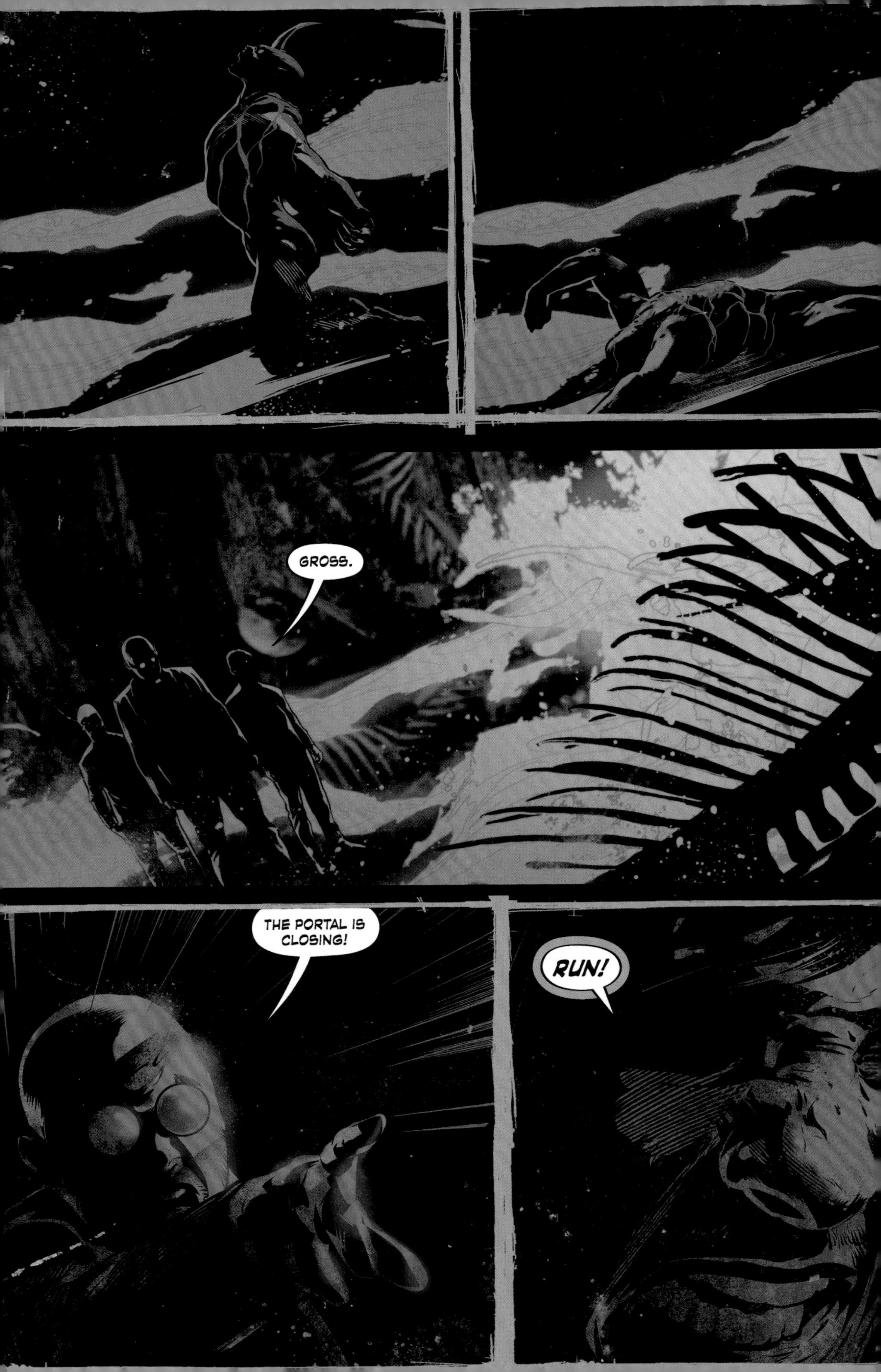
GROSS.
THE PORTAL IS CLOSING!
RUN!

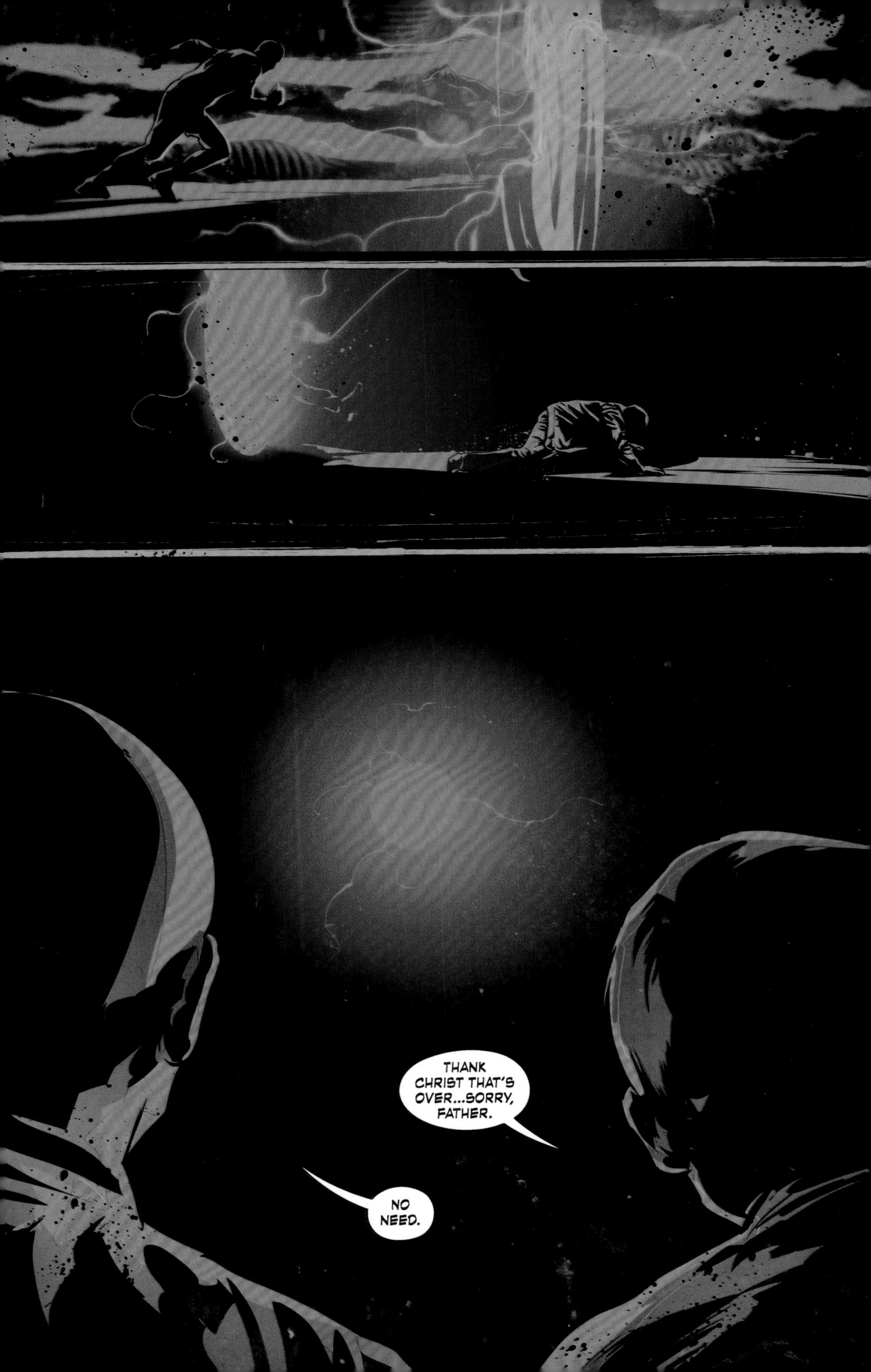
THANK CHRIST THAT'S OVER...SORRY, FATHER.
NO NEED.

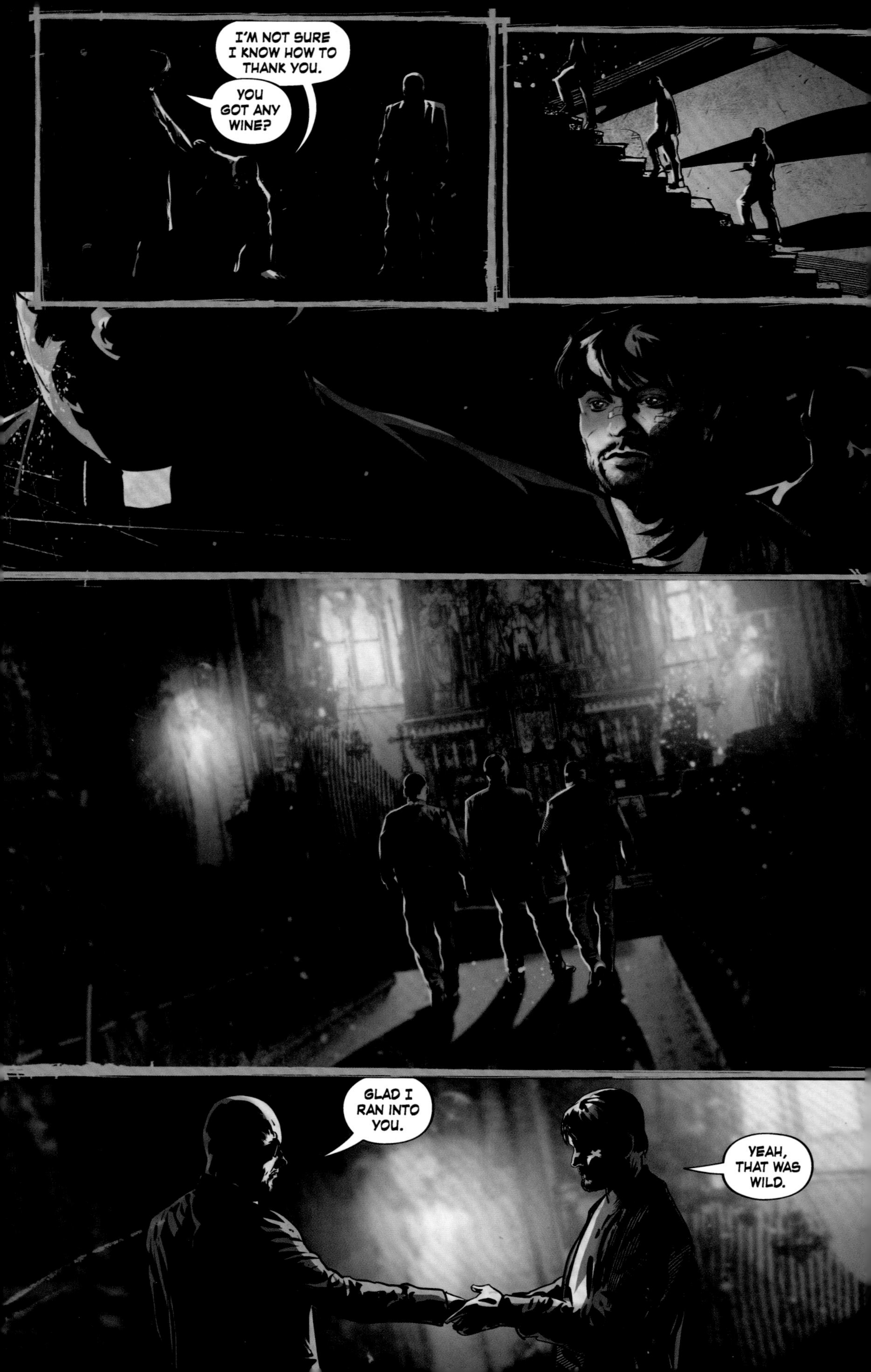
I'M NOT SURE I KNOW HOW TO THANK YOU.
YOU GOT ANY WINE?
GLAD I RAN INTO YOU.
YEAH, THAT WAS WILD.

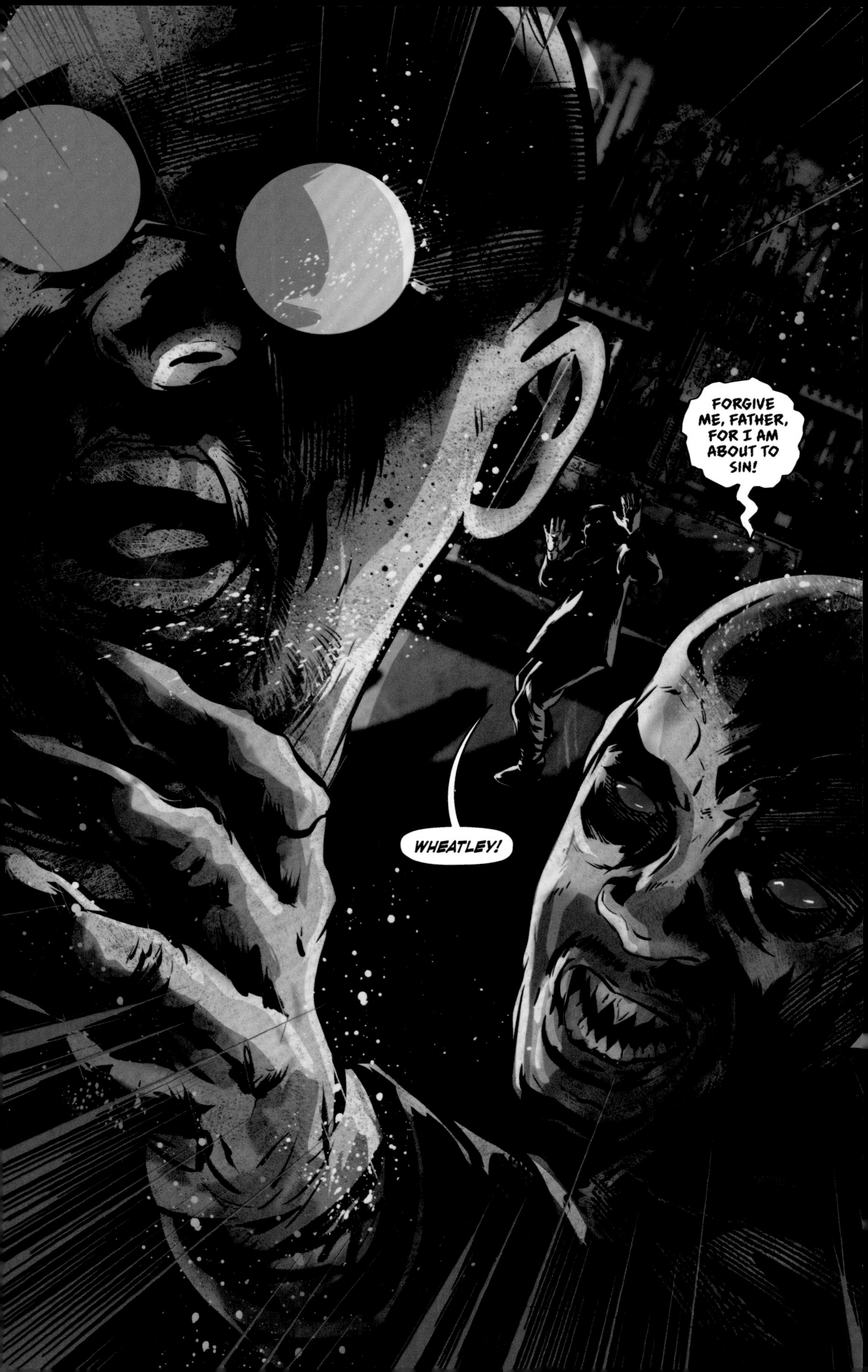
FORGIVE ME, FATHER, FOR I AM ABOUT TO SIN!
WHEATLEY!

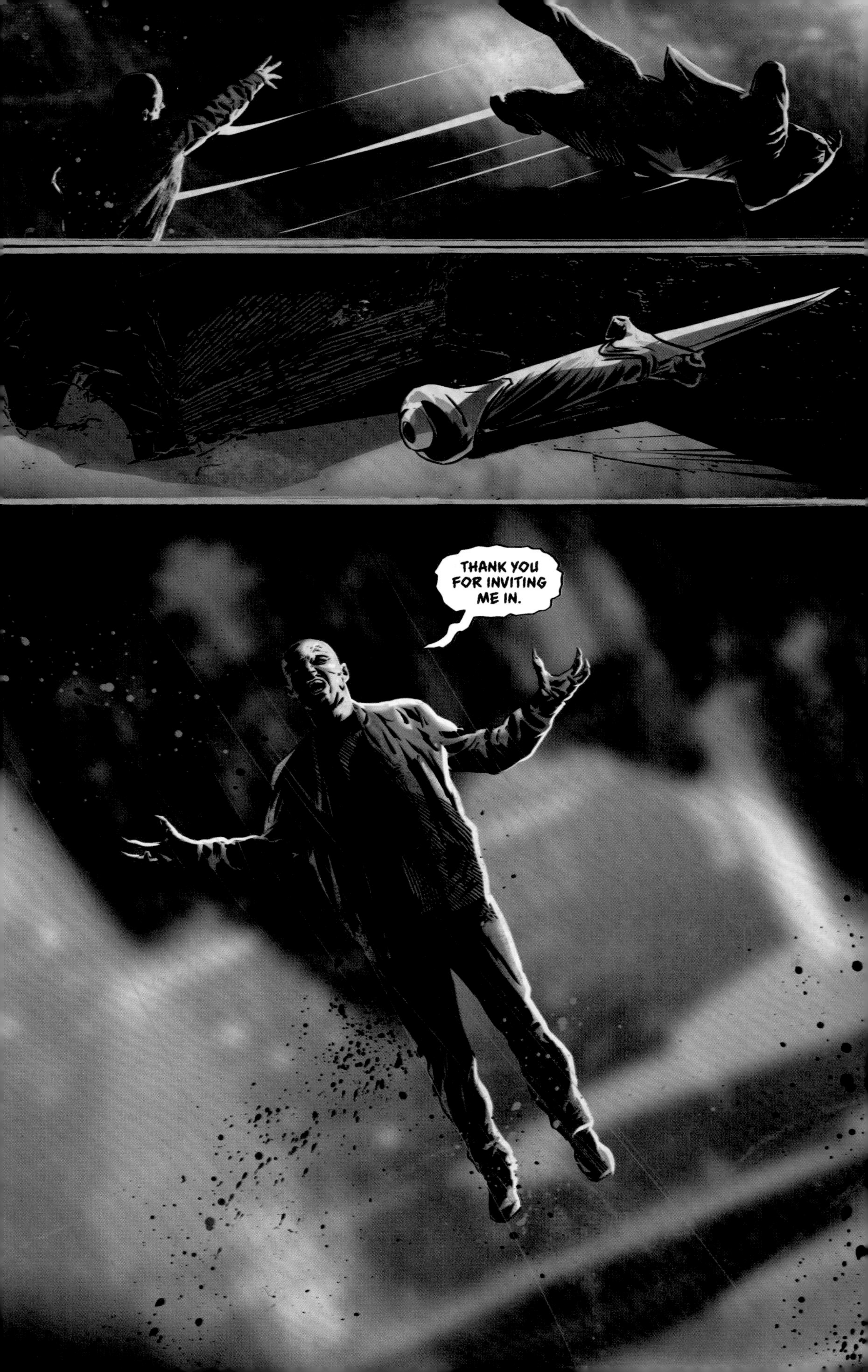
THANK YOU FOR INVITING ME IN.

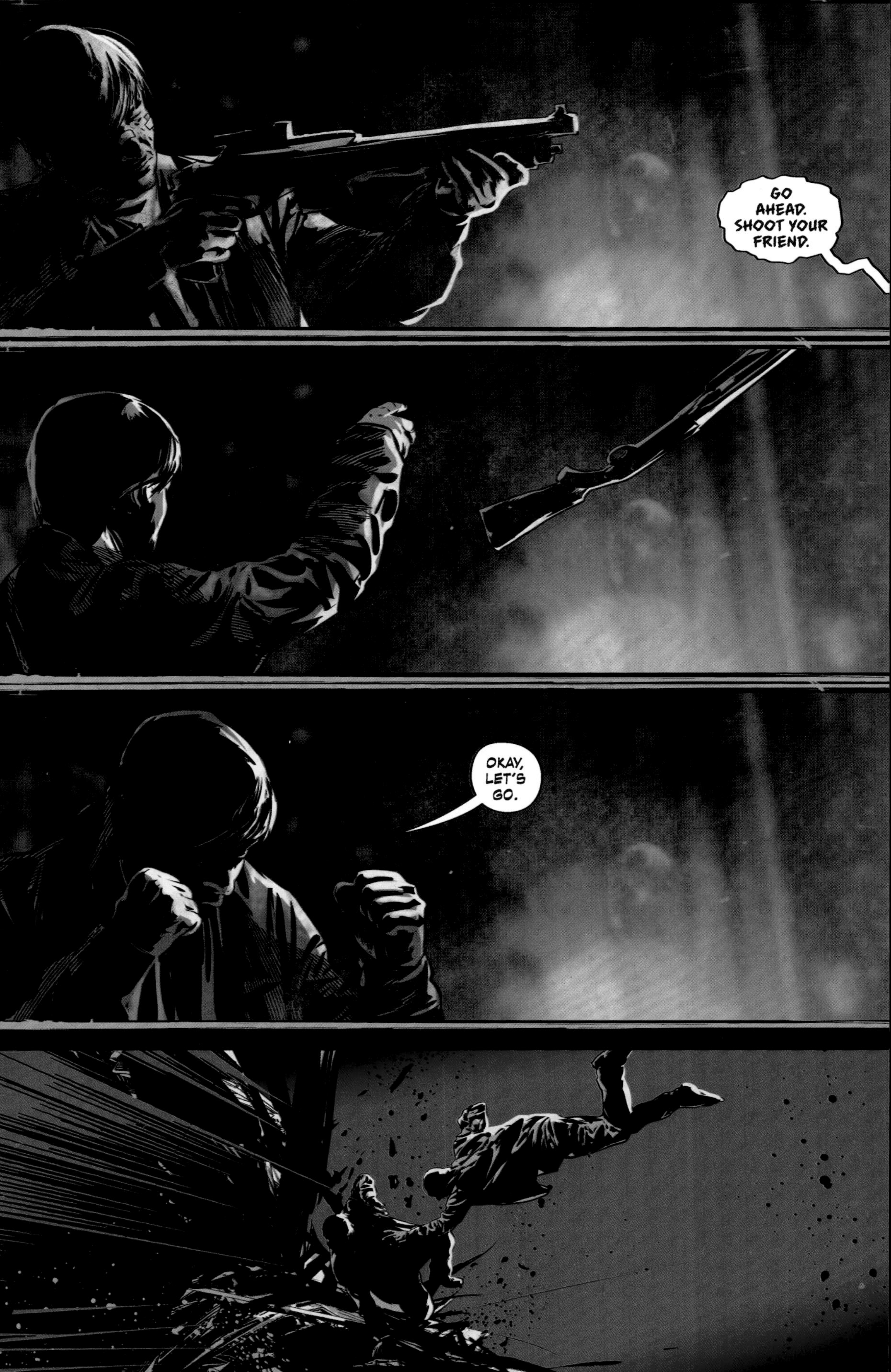
GO AHEAD. SHOOT YOUR FRIEND.
OKAY, LET'S GO.

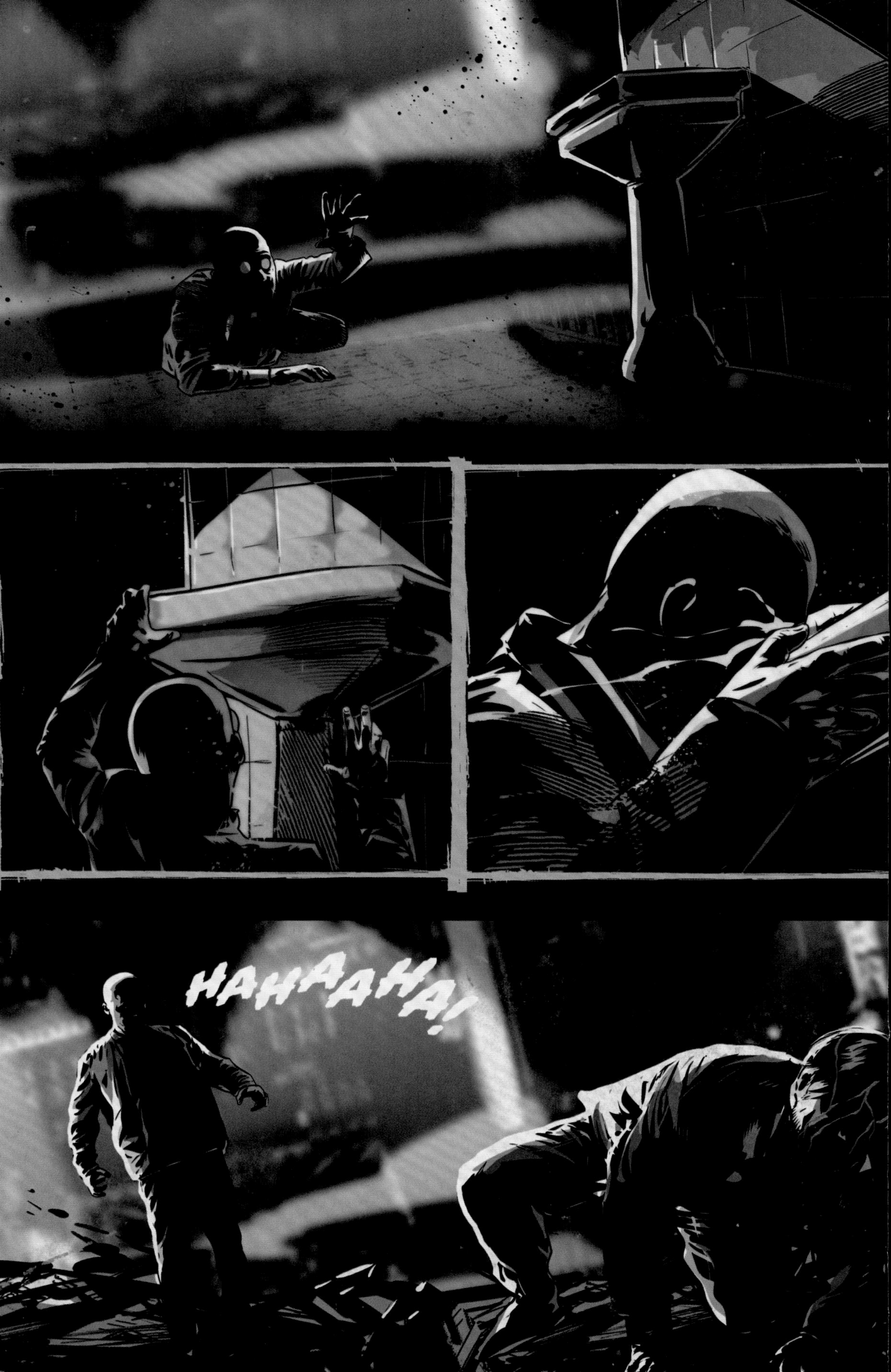
HAHAAAHA!

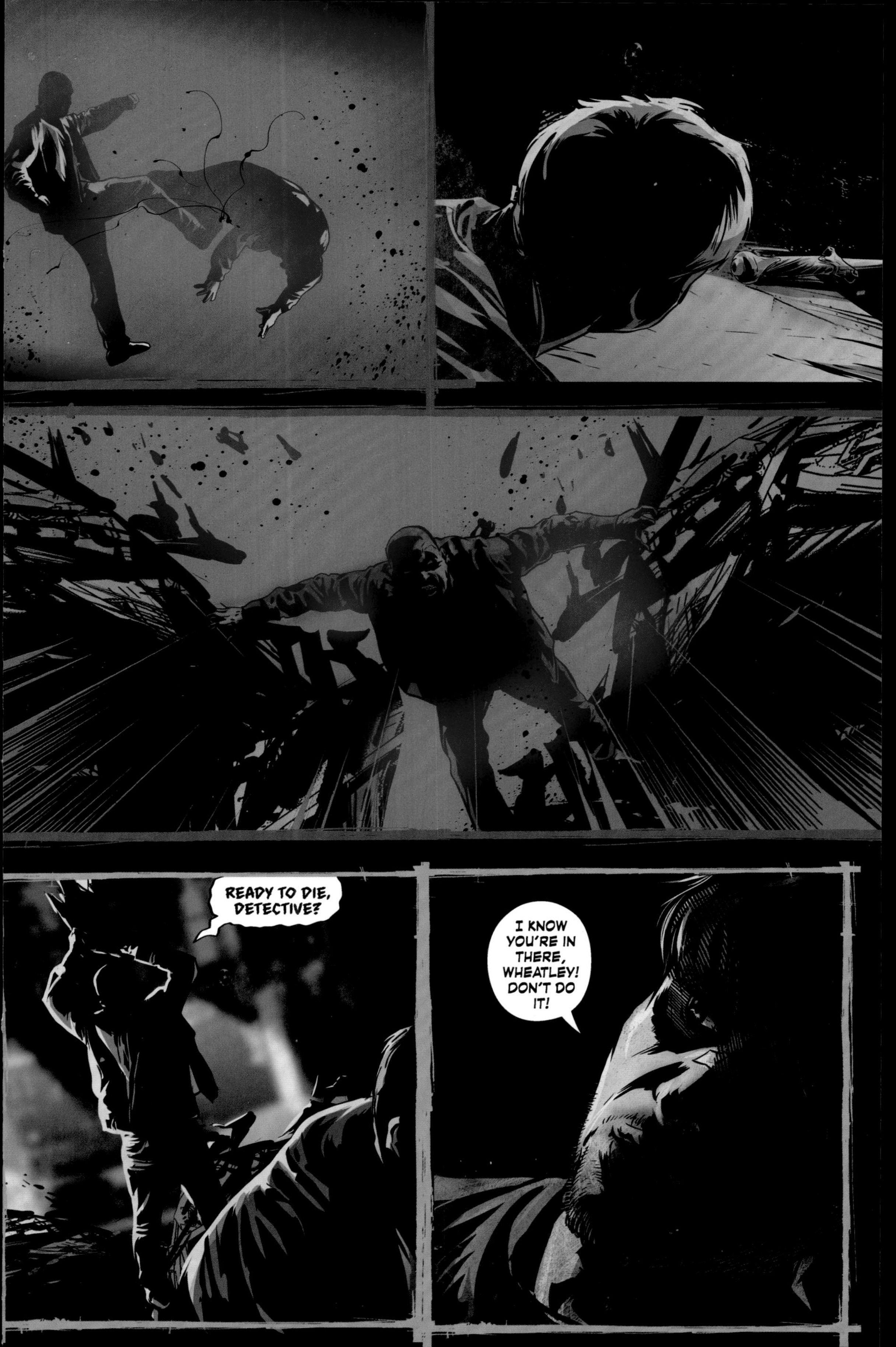
READY TO DIE, DETECTIVE?
I KNOW YOU'RE IN THERE, WHEATLEY! DON'T DO IT!

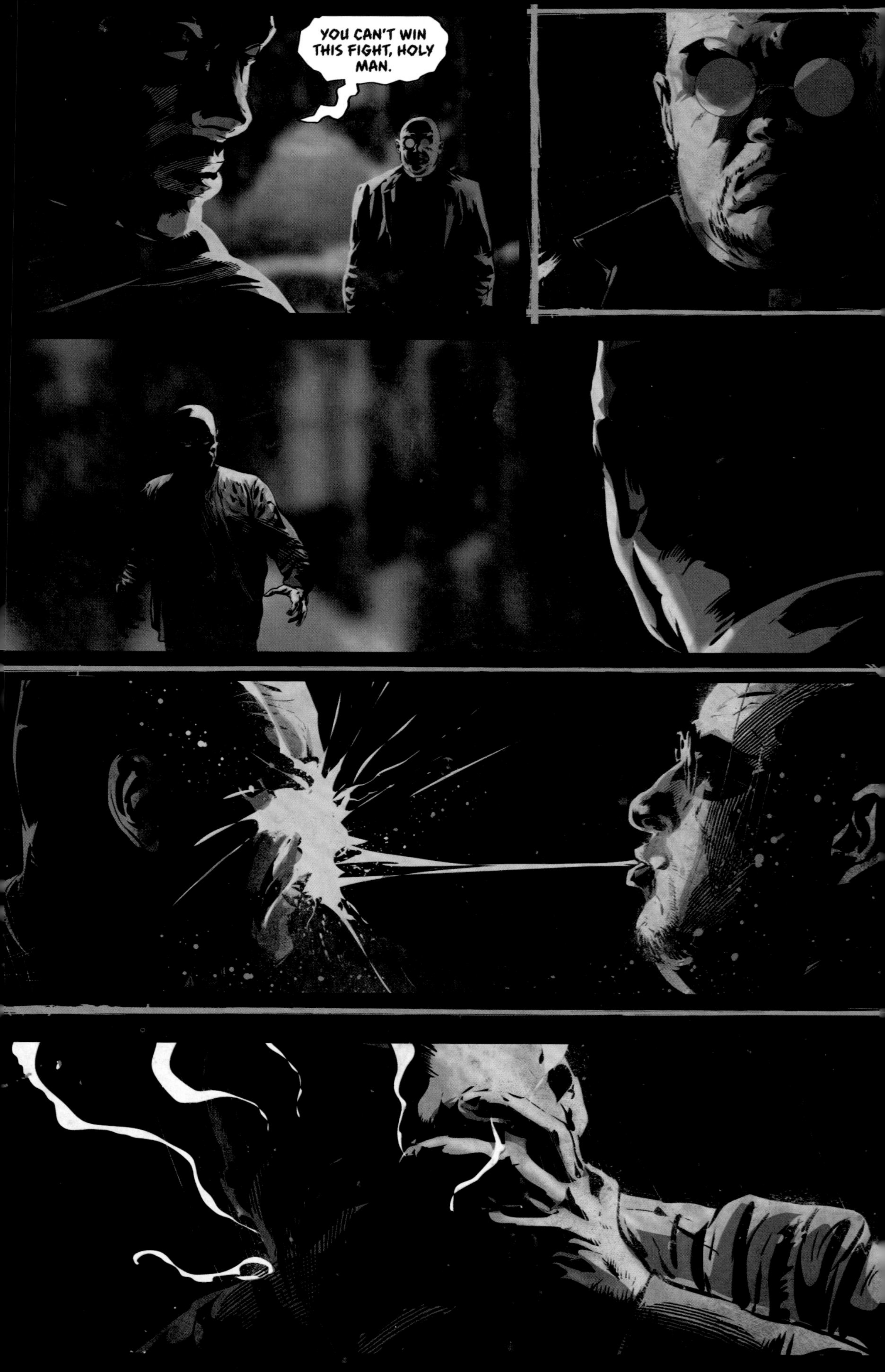
YOU CAN'T WIN THIS FIGHT, HOLY MAN.

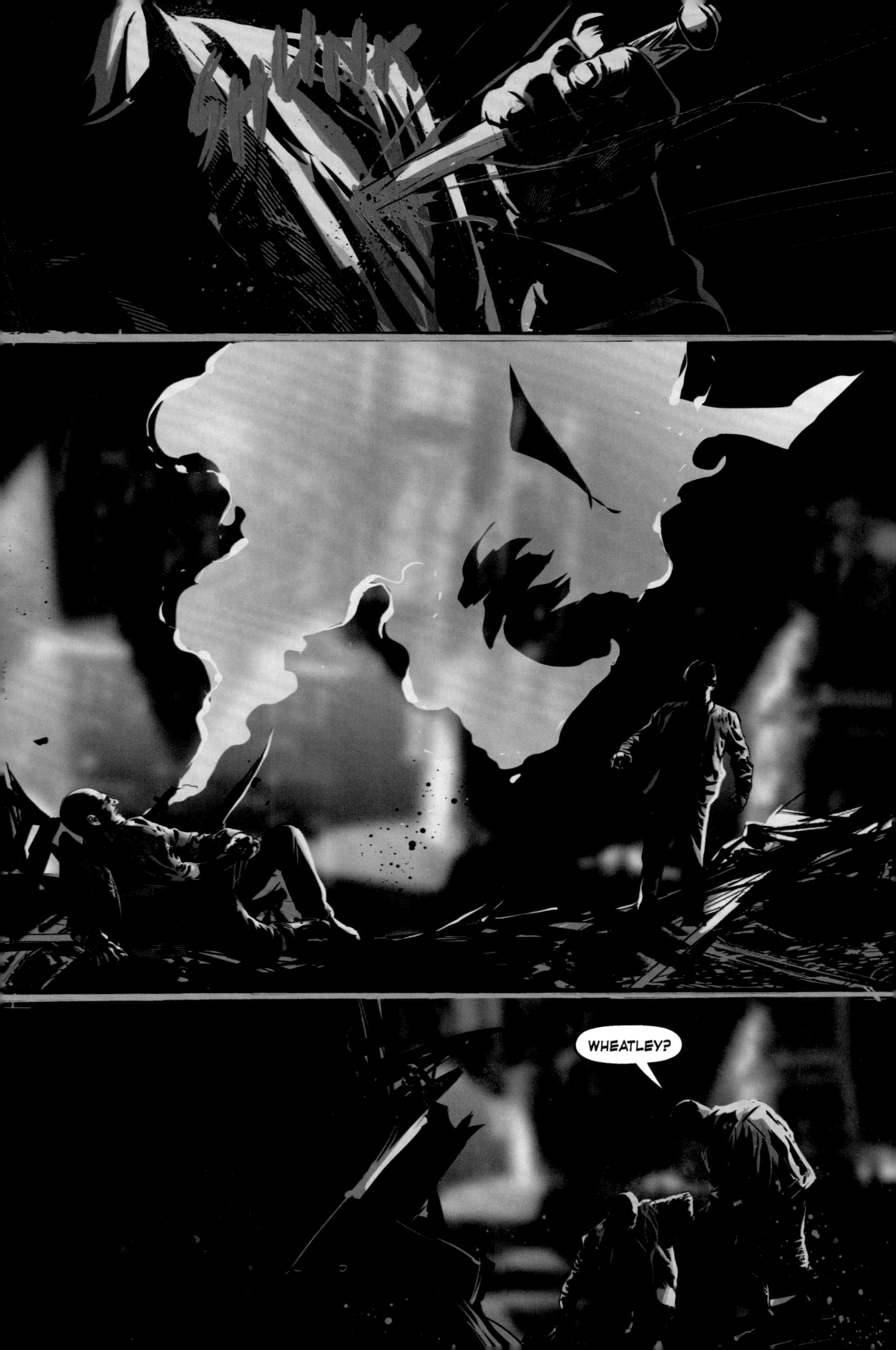
WHEATLEY?

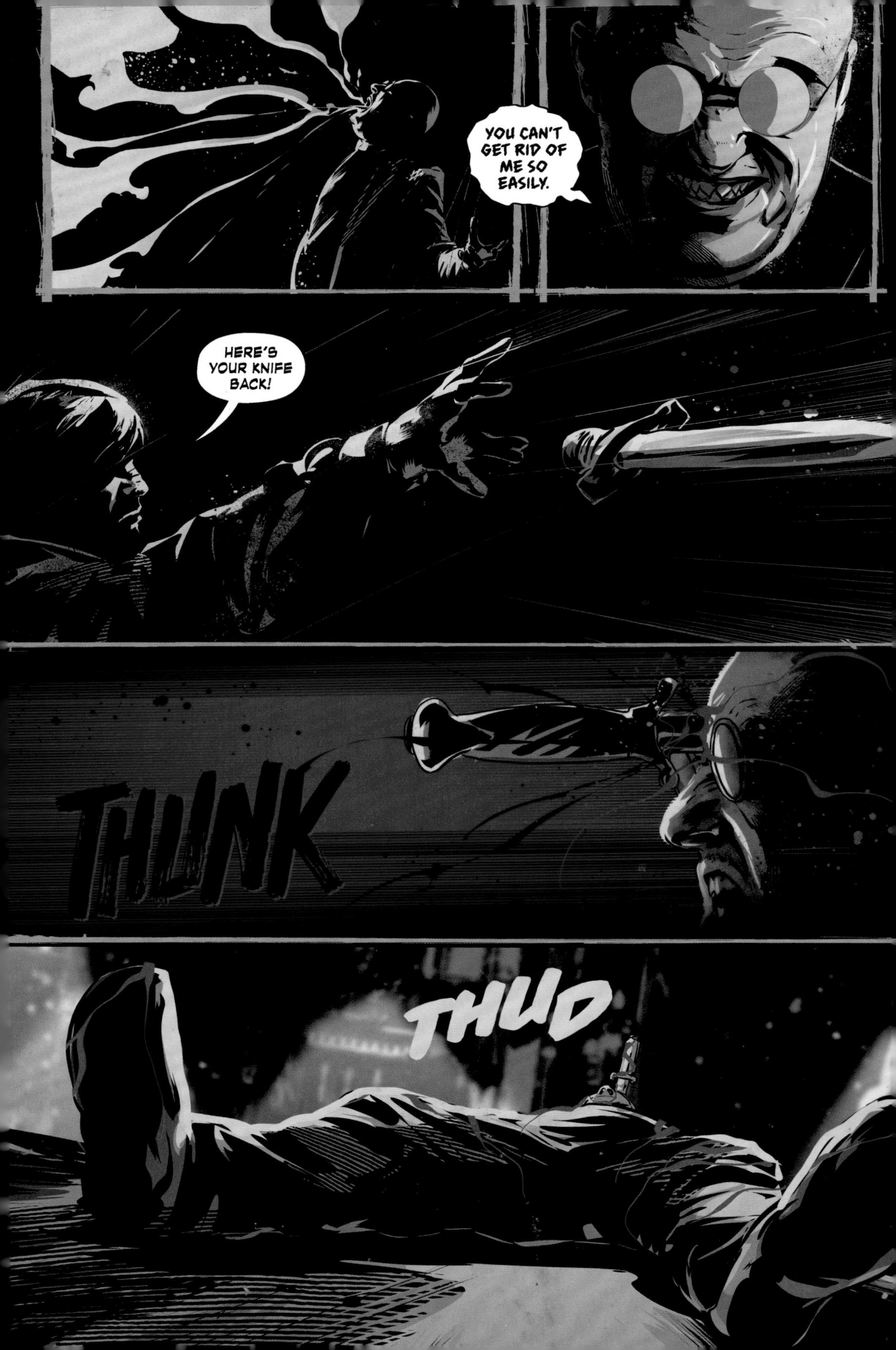
YOU CAN'T GET RID OF ME SO EASILY.
HERE'S YOUR KNIFE BACK!
THUNK
THUD

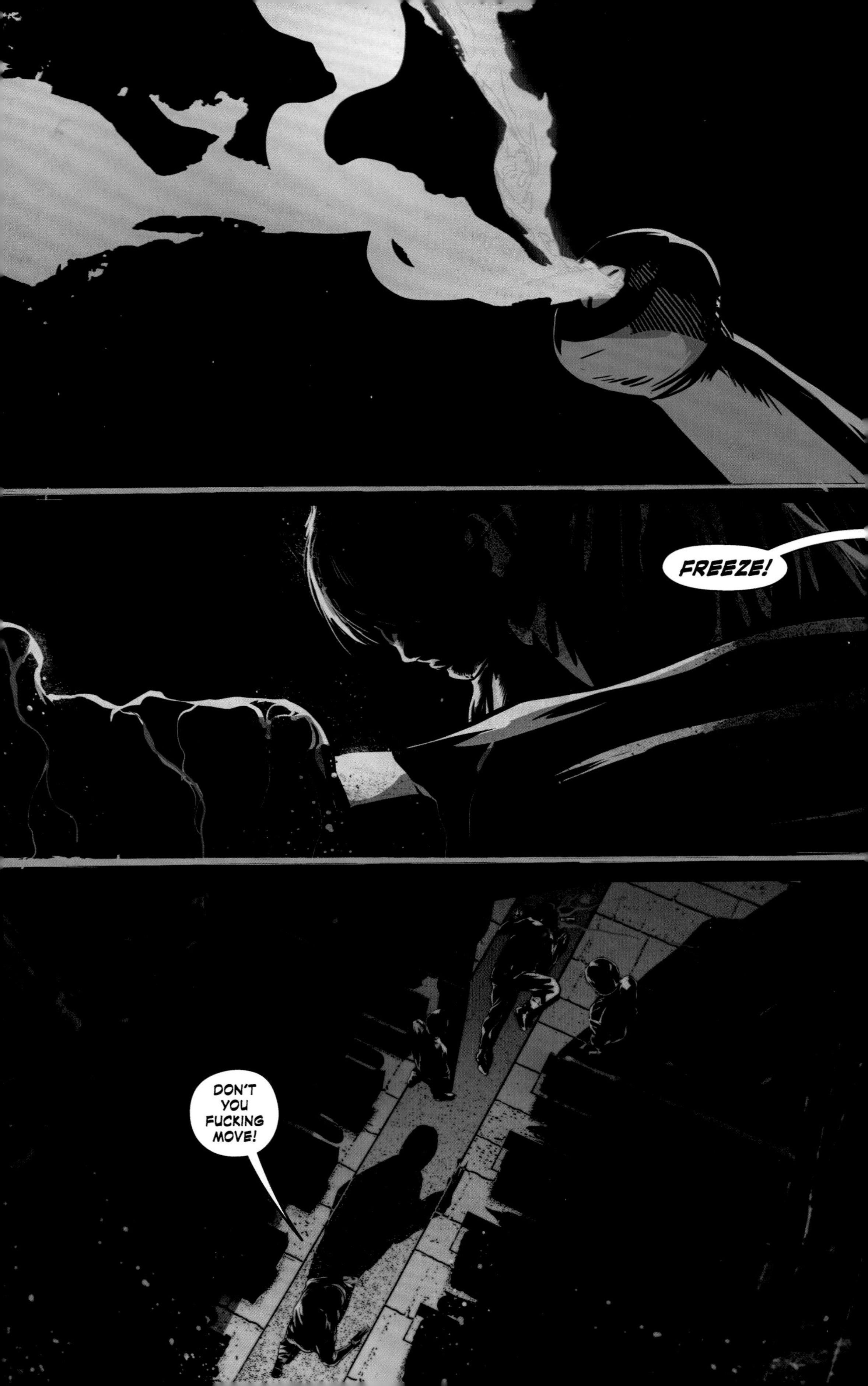
FREEZE!
DON'T YOU FUCKING MOVE!

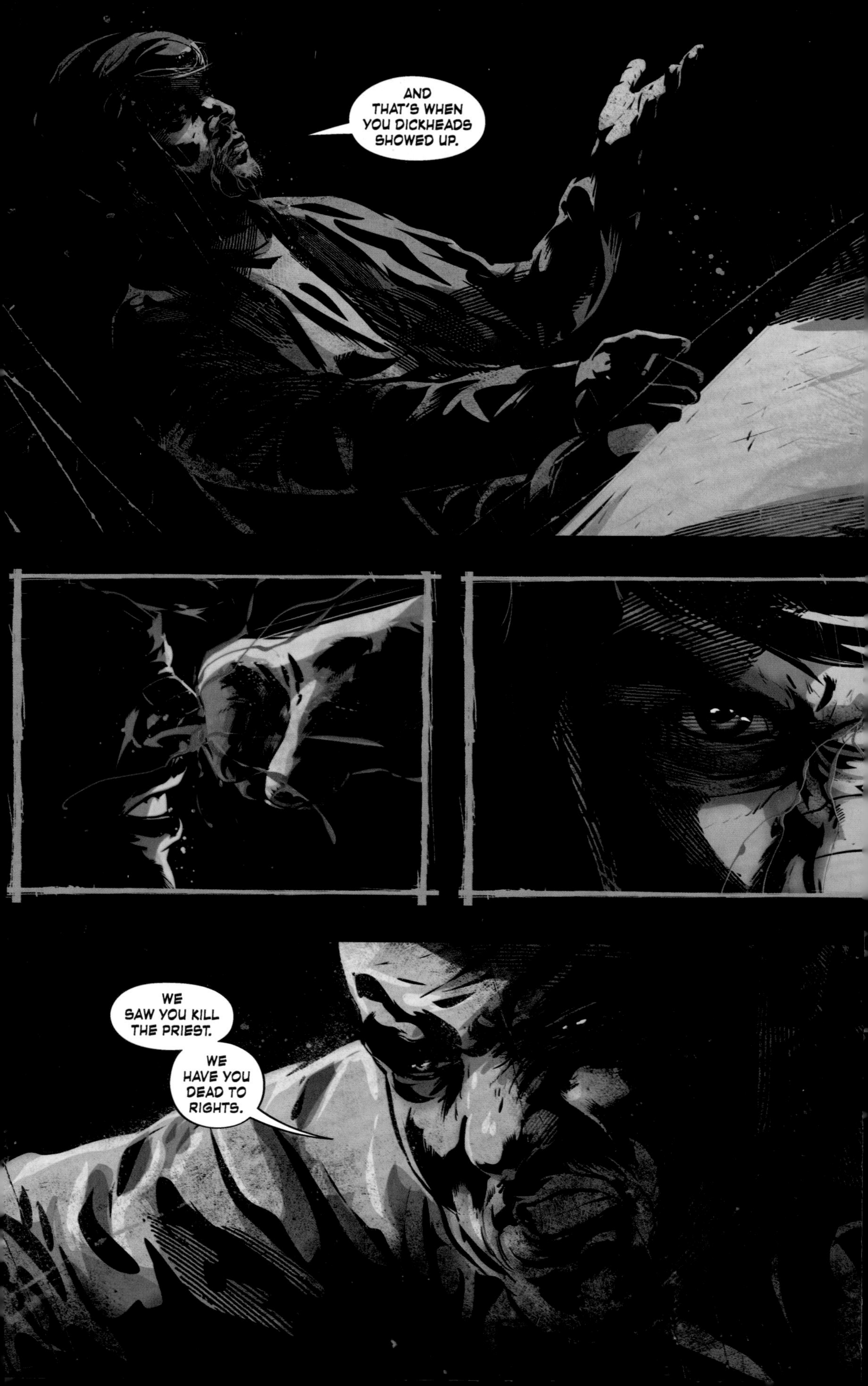
AND THAT'S WHEN YOU DICKHEADS SHOWED UP.
WE SAW YOU KILL THE PRIEST.
WE HAVE YOU DEAD TO RIGHTS.

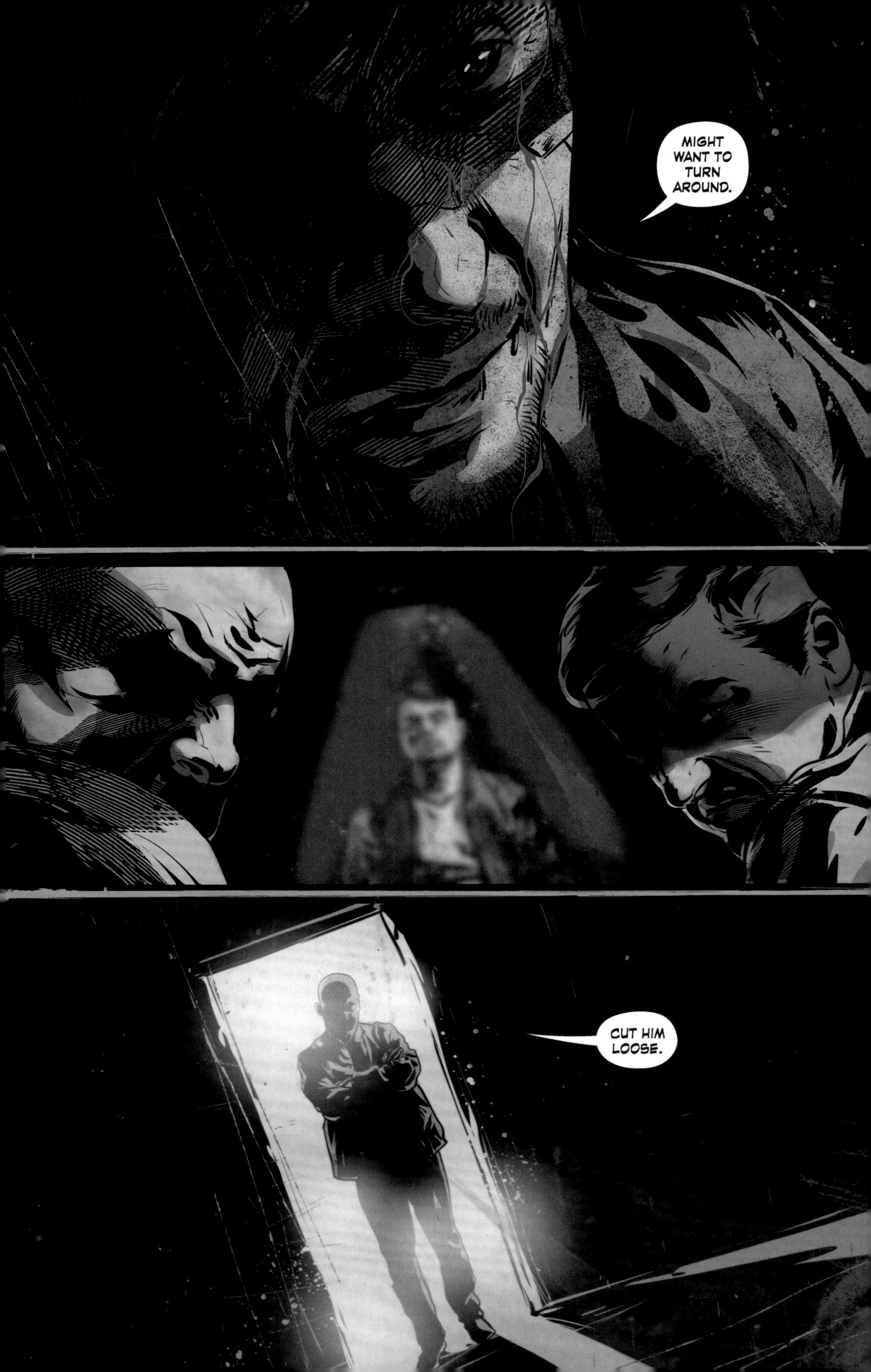
MIGHT WANT TO TURN AROUND.
CUT HIM LOOSE.

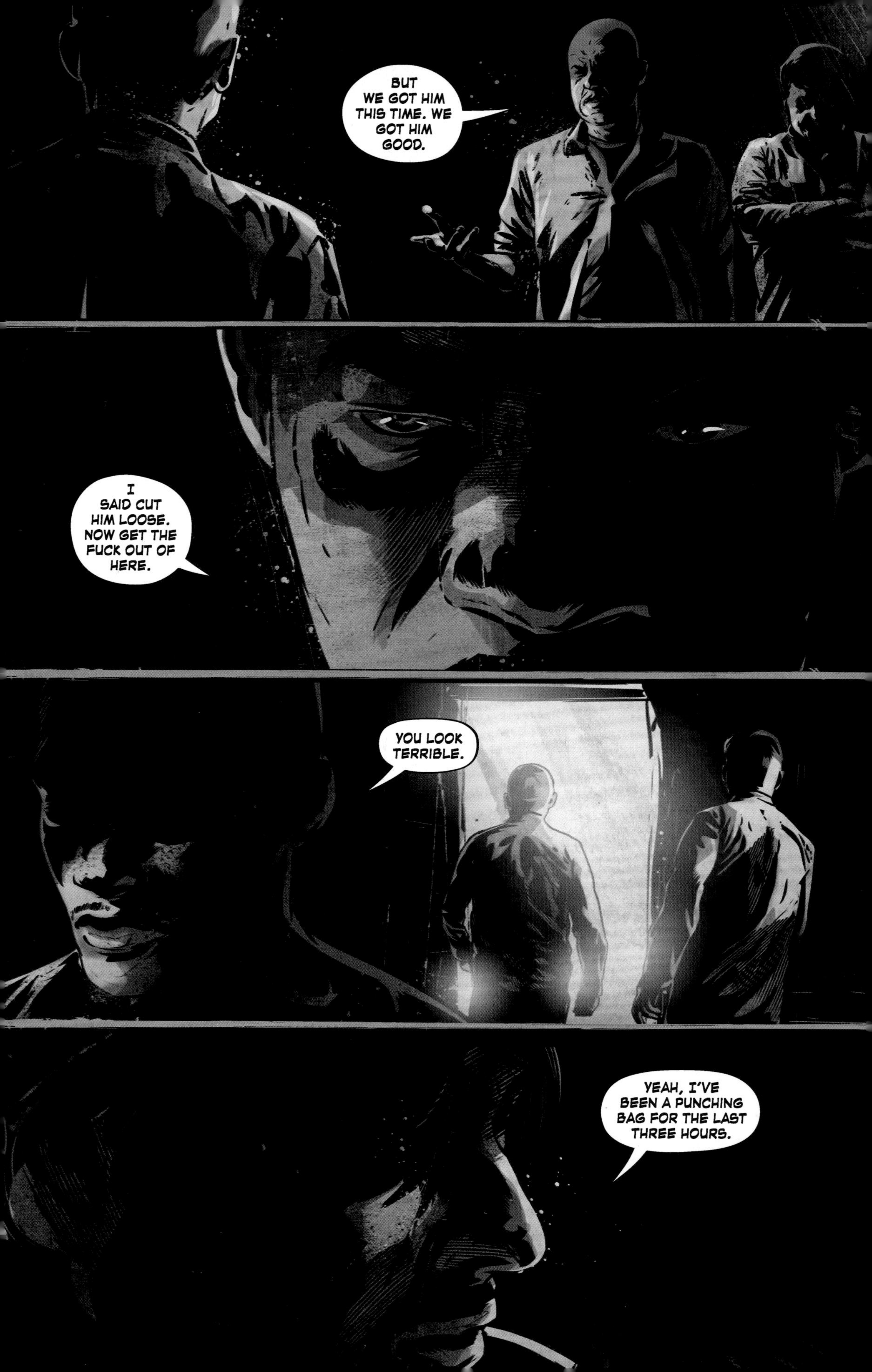
BUT WE GOT HIM THIS TIME. WE GOT HIM GOOD.
I SAID CUT HIM LOOSE. NOW GET THE FUCK OUT OF HERE.
YOU LOOK TERRIBLE.
YEAH, I'VE BEEN A PUNCHING BAG FOR THE LAST THREE HOURS.

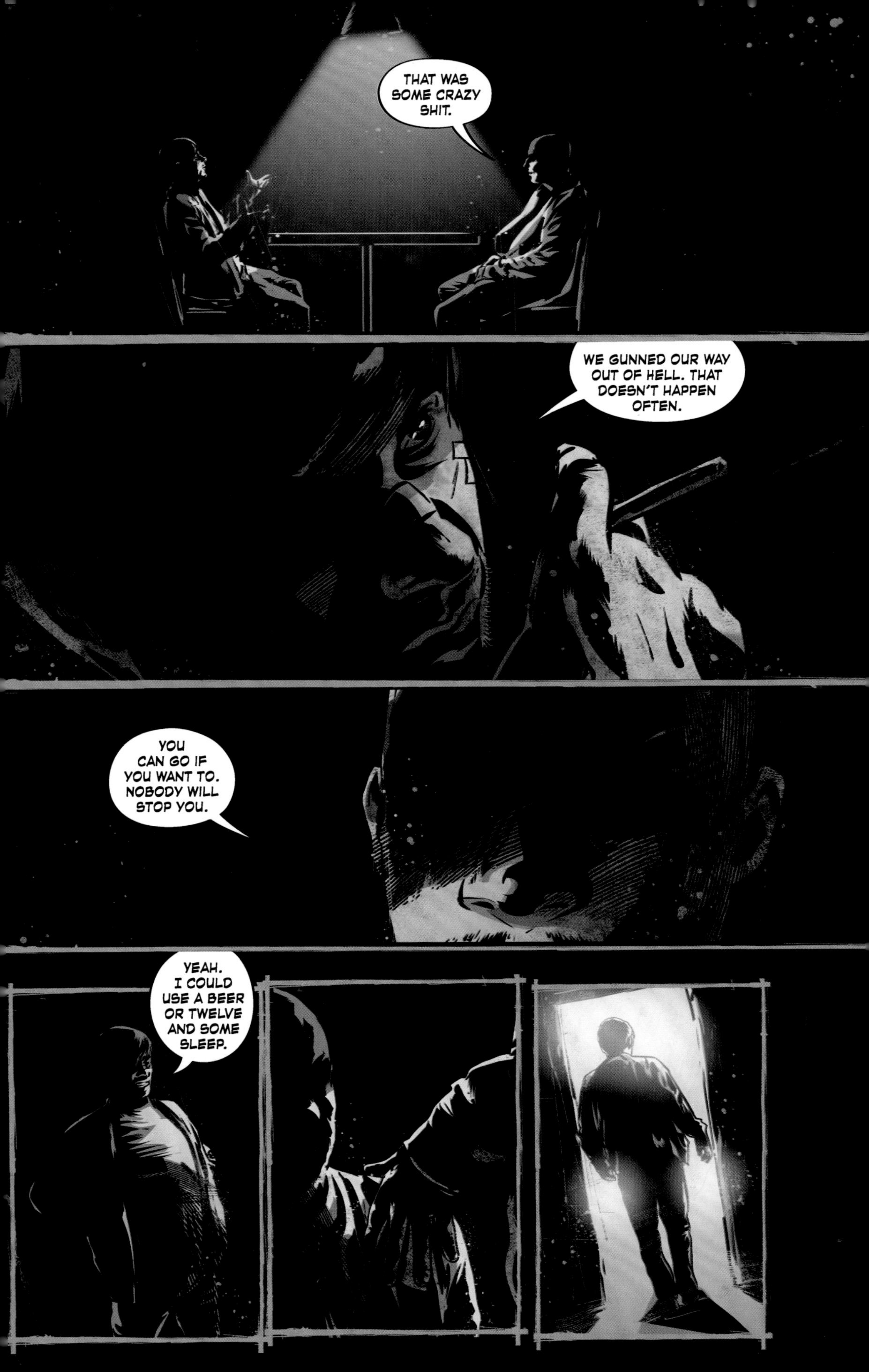
THAT WAS SOME CRAZY SHIT.
WE GUNNED OUR WAY OUT OF HELL. THAT DOESN'T HAPPEN OFTEN.
YOU CAN GO IF YOU WANT TO. NOBODY WILL STOP YOU.
YEAH. I COULD USE A BEER OR TWELVE AND SOME SLEEP.

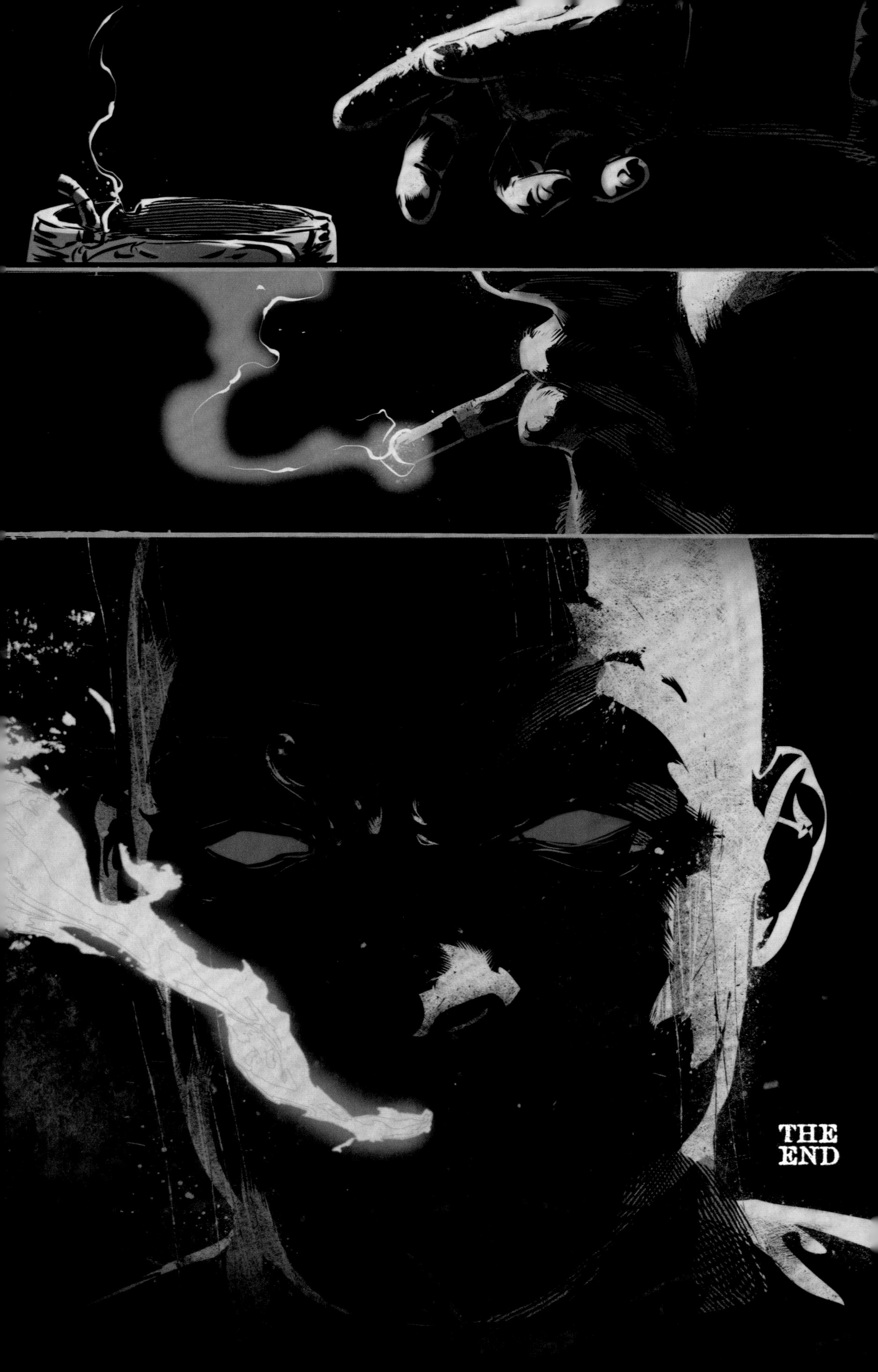
THE
END

CRIMINAL MACABRE™

SPIRIT OF THE DEMON

PROCESS WORK

SPLASH with insets: Straight on shot of Cal sitting at an interrogation table under the hot lights. He looks like Hell, beat to a pulp. Hanging over him are two large cop shadows.

1) COP (off panel)
Come on, McDonald. We have you dead to rights.

2) CAL
What you think happened didn't happen. You got the wrong guy.

3) COP 2(off panel)
Bullshit. We caught you red handed. Spill it.

Inset One: Close on Cal. He looks like shit.

4) CAL
Where's Wheatley? He knows what happened.

Inset Two: Reveal Cops. They both look like goons in shabby suits.

5) COP 1
Wheatley is fighting for his life in the hospital.

6) COP 2
Tell us about the priest.

Panel 1: Cal looks at the cops.

1) CAL

Wait a second…you think I killed the…and
hurt Wheatley? You guys stupid or what?

Panel 2: BAM! A cop fist slams into Cal's face.

Panel 3: Cop 1 leans in.

2) COP 1

You wanna start talking or you want more of that?

Panel 4: Cal wipes the blood from his mouth with his sleeve.

3) CAL

Okay, relax. Adam 12.

Panel 5: Close on bloody Cal.

4) CAL

I'll tell you everything I know.

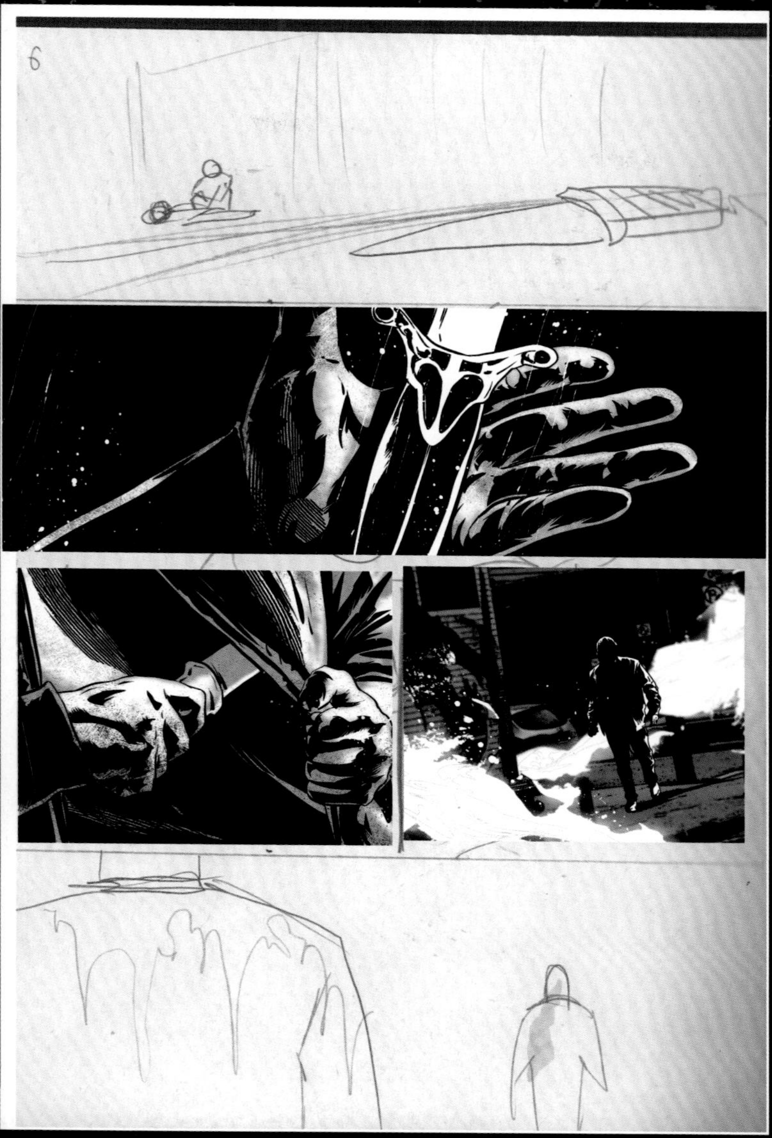
6

Panel 1: Cal is kneeling now examining her. Cal looks to the right and sees the KNIFE on the ground.

Panel 2: Close on knife in Cal's hand. It is an ornate sacrificial knife and looks ancient.

1) CAL
What's this?

Panel 3: Cal tucks the knife inside his jacket.

2) CAL
Mine now.

Panel 4: Cal leaves the alley looking sober all of a sudden.

Panel 5: A large shape peers from the alley following him.

Panel 1: Cal dials his phone with one hand and lights a smoke with the other. Looks hand rolled.

Panel 2: At his home, Wheatley is in bed as his cellphone rings and rattles on the side table. It's late night.

1) WHEATLEY

Who the hell?

Panel 3: Cal exhales and mock smiles as he speaks into the phone.

2) CAL

Hey, Wheatley! You sleeping?

Panel 4: Wheatley is sitting up now and pissed as he talks into his cell phone.

3) WHEATLEY

It's the middle of the goddamn night, Cal!

Panel 5: Cal speaks into the phone.

4) CAL

There's a body in the alley between CVS and
Urban Outfitters on Ventura. I didn't do it.

Panel 6: Cal hangs up.

Panel 1: Cal looks over at the window next to the front door as he hears something.

1) SOUNDFX

Snap!

Panel 2: Cal pulls out his gun.

Panel 3: Cal peers out the window.

2) CAL

Nothing.

3) SOUNDFX

Crunch!

Panel 4: Cal stands on the front porch gun at ready.

4) CAL

Who's there?

Panel 5: A shape begins to emerge from shadows.

Panel 1: Inside Cal sits at his desk with the knife in front of him on the blotter. The priest stands a bit away. He's a freakin' big priest.

1) CAL
Have a seat. Can I get you a drink?

2) PRIEST
No thank you. I won't be long.

Panel 2: On Cal, shooting straight.

3) CAL
You want to tell me what happened in the alley?

Panel 3: On Priest.

4) PRIEST
I was doing the Lord's work.

Panel 4: Cal looks blank. Says nothing here.

Panel 5: Now Cal is talking.

5) CAL
Can you be a little more specific? I saw that thing you killed. That was not human.

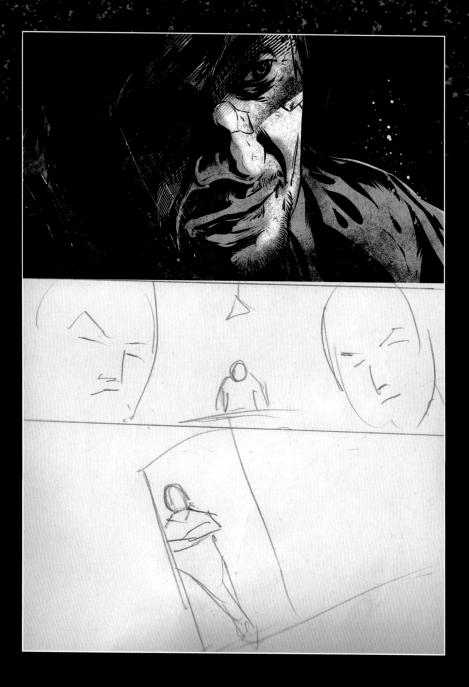

Panel 1: Cal bleeds and looks at the cops and smiles with bloody teeth. He's looking right past the cops.

1) CAL
Might want to turn around.

Panel 2: The two cops look behind them and see…

Panel 3: Wheatley stands in the doorway, arm in a sling, shoulder wrapped.

2) WHEATLEY
Cut him loose.